BLESSED BEYOND ALL MEANS

BLESSED BEYOND ALL MEANS
FROM RURAL GEORGIA TO THE CORRIDORS OF POWER

GEORGE WATSON CAMP

INTERVIEW
You™

Published by Interview You
Athens, Georgia

Text design by The Adsmith
www.theadsmith.com

*Grateful acknowledgement is made to the Special Collections
Department, Georgia State University Library for photographs as
noted in this text. All others are family and official photographs
from the personal collection of George W. Camp.*

ISBN 0-9773365-6-5
Printed in the United States of America

For My Family

Contents

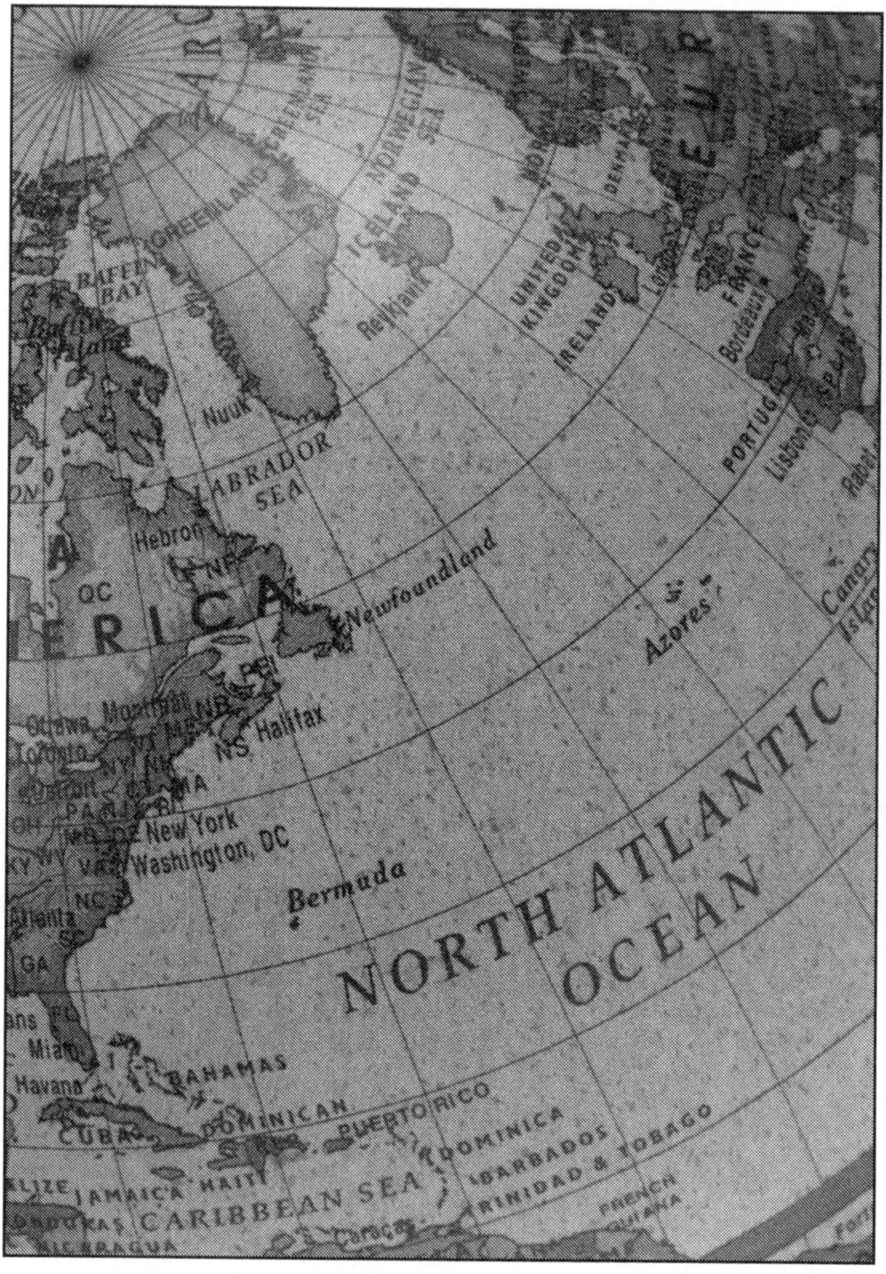

GREENLAND
NORWEGIAN SEA
ICELAND
Reykjavik
BAFFIN BAY
UNITED KINGDOM
IRELAND
FRANCE
Bordeaux
PORTUGAL
Lisbon
Nuuk
LABRADOR SEA
Hebron
QC
Newfoundland
Azores
NS Halifax
Montreal
Ottawa
Toronto
New York
Washington, DC
Bermuda
NORTH ATLANTIC OCEAN
Atlanta
GA
Miami
Havana
BAHAMAS
CUBA
DOMINICAN
PUERTO RICO
DOMINICA
BARBADOS
TRINIDAD & TOBAGO
JAMAICA
HAITI
CARIBBEAN SEA

CHAPTER 1

The Early Camps

Do you remember hearing any of your grandparents describe their lives?

My dad, I think my dad was about ten years old when his father died and my grandmother raised all those boys and her daughter by herself on the farm. I don't remember too much about them, but on my mother's side, I remember visiting with my grandmother and granddad and then he'd take us riding in the buggy, and it was raining and cold and snow on the ground, and we'd like to freeze. I know one day we went to Canton to buy groceries. I was a little bitty fellow, but I just barely remember it. That's about the only time I ever remember being with him. But when he got old his last days, I didn't see much of him.

Do you know anything about the Camp family history? Do you know, say, when the first family member would have come to America?

They came, I've been told, in the 1600s. And one family, I've been told, had twenty-three sons and one daughter, and that's where they started and scattered all over the United States.

That's a pretty healthy start.

Yeah, pretty healthy start. So I met people all over the country, Camps, or someone saying, "My maiden name was Camp," or something like that, and I'd discuss it with them, and they'd all refer back to that family name with twenty-three sons and one daughter, every one of them.

Interesting. Do you know where they came from?

Europe, Germany, and I don't know where.

What about where they came to?

Virginia. Settled in Virginia.

And do you know how your branch of the Camp family got to Georgia?

Yes. They came from England to Virginia. That's where it was.

From England, you said?

Europe.

Have you heard any stories about them getting from Virginia to Georgia?

No. I understand my grandfather was raised somewhere in the north Georgia area. Near the Tennessee line. And I don't know anything about his family.

So they migrated south a little bit from there. What about your parents? You were all so busy; I don't know if you had much spare time—did they ever tell you stories about, for instance, how they met?

No, they did not. I think my mama was seventeen when they married. I was born when she was eighteen. Daddy was five years older than my mother. And they didn't tell me much about that.

And they didn't talk much about their childhood, either one of them?

No, of course, they were both born and raised on a farm. That's all they knew. All they knew was farming and canning. No money, very little money back in those days. Had plenty to eat.

So more similar to your childhood, more similar than your children's childhood is to yours. There's quite a difference between your childhood and your children's—

No comparison at all. No comparison.

Well, your parents' childhood and your childhood were more similar, probably.

Right, right. Sometimes they laugh, my boys and grandchildren, they laugh at me when I tell them I walked four miles to school.

So you probably don't know, then, anything about any experiences they had living through wars or being in the military.

My great-grandfather was killed during the War Between the States. He's buried at Crossroads Cemetery. It's near Acworth. That's about all I know about that.

Really. Have you ever been there?

Oh, yeah, I've been there, and I've seen the grave. That was my daddy's grandfather.

Your great-grandfather.

Uh, huh.

And so you knew that, and that was obviously probably spoken about with respect, but you didn't really hear any stories about his life. Do you know how your mother made the great biscuits you've mentioned?

How she made her biscuits?

Yes, yes.

See that thing sitting right up there? [Pointing into the kitchen, towards a large, long, flat wooden bowl, shown below]

Oh, let me see. Let's go look at it.

I don't know what you call it.

So you have the wooden bowl that she made them in and what did she do, she put the—

She'd put whatever she was going to put in the bowl and stir with her hands. And then when she got it all set up, she'd cut out the biscuits, pat them a little bit and put them in the pan. Cook them. And they were good, too.

Are there any other family traditions in terms of cooking or recipes that you remember or that people in the family talked about?

She passed all the recipes down. Martha's got a lot of them, and my grandchildren have got some of them. My sister and all have them.

Cooking wasn't your area of expertise. But they are around—somebody in the family has them.

Oh, yeah.

CHAPTER 2

First of Seven

So now let's begin with your life, George Watson Camp. Let's begin at the beginning. Tell me about where you were born.

I was born May the third 1920 in a small house on my grandmother's farm about a block from where she lived. It was, I am told, coming a flood that day—of course this was a farm four miles out of Dallas, Georgia. And my mother and dad told me that they asked my uncle to go get the doctor. And there was no bridges and he rode a horse and his horse had to swim through a creek to get to the doctor. But evidently the doctor got there in time. [Laughter] So that's what happened on that day. But that was a long, long time ago. [Laughter]

What family was there as you arrived?

Only my mother and my grandmother, I think, on the Camp side. I was first of seven surviving children.

Can you name them, in order, maybe?

[Gets out briefcase and finds prepared material]

Nice preparation!

Yeah. My second brother born after me was born on March 11, 1922. He's two years younger than I am. Two years younger, so he was born in 1922. William Maddox Camp, that's my brother.

And then the next one was Octavia Beatrice Camp, sister, born in 1924. And when she was about four or five months old, she took the whooping cough, and we lost her. So she's deceased.

Then after her was Ruby Estelle Camp. She was born February 7th, 1928. And the next one was Nick Donald Camp. He was born April 13th, 1932. Then Juanita Camp was born February 25th, 1934. And Ozelle Camp, was born May 4th, 1937. And then Patsy Jo Camp, July 4th, 1940. That's the Camp family.

Whooping cough has just about been eradicated now. Do you remember the events surrounding your sister's illness?

Yes, I remember; I had it also. We had moved from the Camp plantation, so-to-speak, three miles in a different direction. And my daddy was in the transfer business back in those days with a T-model Ford. There's only three things that I actually, or four, that I remember at this location. I remember living there.

You called it the Camp plantation. Was that the family home, the home-place?

My dad's mother's home. And when we moved there I remember living at this location, and I remember having the whooping cough. Of course, I was very young. And I remember when Beatrice died. I remember that.

And did that happen at home?

Yeah, that happened at home. No hospitals then, in that part of the country.

And doctors came to the house, too.

Yeah, doctors come to the house. And Daddy bought an Overland automobile, and I remember this—he was out there trying to start it. You had to crank it. No batteries then—you had to crank it. And he broke his arm, and that scared me to death. He kicked it. And I remember him breaking his arm.

And on another occasion, a friend of Daddy's killed a man. And he was trying to get away from the law. And my mama cooked a flour sack full of food for him. And I was amazed watching them, you know. And when she handed it to him, he and Daddy left in his T-model truck. And Daddy didn't get back until the next day sometime. It was dark when they left. But to this day, as long as he lived, he never would tell me where he took him. Never heard from him again.

I wonder what was behind the story—your father must have felt it was justified or that his friend wouldn't get justice or something.

I don't know. I do remember him coming to the house. I remember him coming to the house and telling Daddy what happened.

And you were the little one watching it all.

Yes, I was a little one. I guess—what—five years old?

Yes—so that's an early dramatic memory. What do you remember about the house?

It was a farmhouse. Just a two- or three-room house. You sleep and live in the same room. Kitchen was a different room; [we'd] eat and cook in the same room. Nothing like we have today. No electricity. No plumbing. You had to draw your water from a well. Had lamps to see with. So back in those days, no pavement at all, mud. You get out and walk anyplace, you walk in the mud.

Oh. wow. I never thought about that. And so your food—was it mostly what you grew?

Vegetables, mostly. And it's just a period of time I don't remember a lot about the food. I do later. But Daddy was in the transfer business, moving people. Bought a T-model truck. First time I remember my daddy I was setting aside of him on this T-model truck.

And so he helped people moving from one place to another or that sort of thing. I guess any kind of moving.

Flat-bed truck. Flat beds are like this: you have to tie your furniture on. It wasn't much bigger than this. [Indicating the large conference-room table]

Let's talk a little bit more about those days. The house that you moved into when you moved away from your mother's family—you lived there most of the time growing up?

We didn't live there long. You want me to tell you what happened after that?

Yes.

For some reason Daddy evidently wasn't doing too well in the transfer business, so he left and went to Miami.

Miami, Florida?

Yes. This was after Beatrice died. He got a job with the Florida Power and

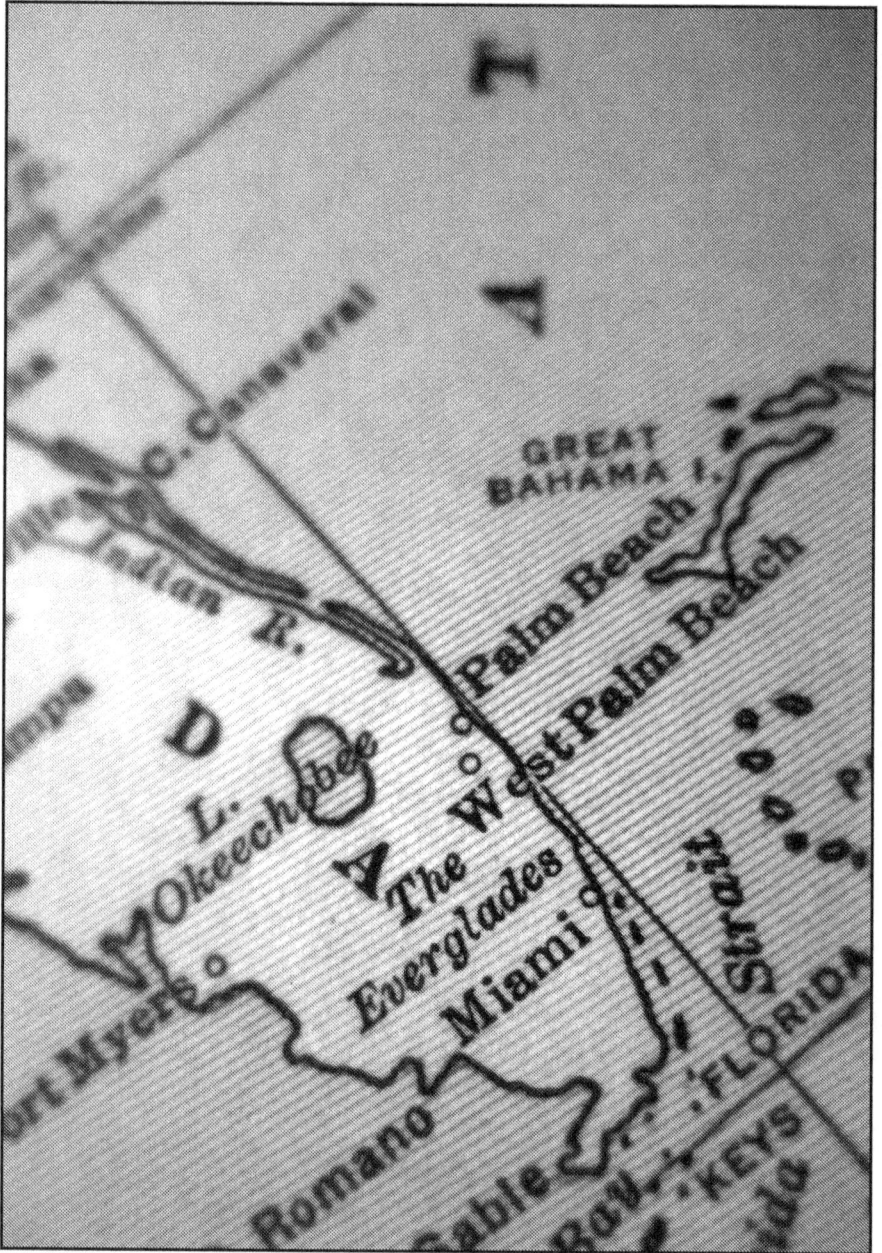

Light. And my mother took my brother, Junior, as we called him, and me on a train, and we went to Miami to live.

Well, that must have been pretty exciting.

'25.

Unusual in those days.

Oh, yeah. I wasn't used to anything like that; we had lights down there. And when we were down there, we had a nice house to live in. And I remember going to the beach, Miami Beach. Nothing out there, just beach.

A lot different than today.

Right. And we'd been down there a few months and a storm or a hurricane came in. 1926. And my daddy let everybody on the street in the house. There were so many people in the house that you couldn't move. I remember walking in between them, black and white, and it was terrible—history says that in '26 the hurricane in Miami was terrible. And after it was over, my mother took my brother and myself and got on the train and come home.

Did she?

She wouldn't stay there anymore.

That once was enough.

Once was enough. So Daddy stayed about three months later, and then he came back. And then that's when we moved back to the homeplace, the farm, the Camp farm. And he started farming, and we lived there the rest of the time that I was home.

CHAPTER 3

Forty-Eight Biscuits

Okay, so this farm you moved to was his parents' place.

My dad's parents.

Was yours the only family there or were there other family members living there too?

My grandmother. Just my grandmother.

So you grew up with your grandmother in the house?

Yes. She lived with us a long time.

That's nice. And so you were approximately how old when you came back from—oh! it was the '26 hurricane. It blew you out of town.

Yes.

So then your father takes up farming.

Right.

And how did that go?

Oh, it liked to kill me. The first winter. It was a terrible winter—ice on the ground, stuff like that. And, of course, we didn't have any money, just getting started. And we had to cut wood for the fireplace and stove, stuff like that. And I was out there, a six-year-old, pulling a cross-cut saw with Daddy, cutting wood.

Really? Six years old!

Yeah. And he said, "Quit riding the saw, son. Quit riding the saw."

Really—

But we managed through the winter. But that was the hardest winter, I guess, of my daddy's life and my mama's because after that we started raising stuff.

Right, because when you came in it would have been fall after the hurricane and you hadn't had a crop.

Hadn't had a crop, and it was rough.

So starting with the cross-cut saw and getting firewood, you probably were involved in much of the farm work through your life.

Completely. Everything, everything. I'll never forget my daddy. I never understood how he could wake up at 3:30 in the morning—3:30 in the morning he'd say, "Son, get up and go feed the mules." Every morning. And, of course, I'd go feed the mules. And when I got back, he'd have a fire started in the wood stove, and Mama'd be in there cooking biscuits. And she'd cook forty-eight biscuits. I'd eat five or six of them myself. [Laughter] When you work from sun up to sun down.

Right, you need that.

You need that.

Wow. And so you had biscuits and did you have butter with them—did you have any meat with them?

Oh, yeah. Daddy had, always, five or six hogs. We'd kill five, six, or more hogs. We had plenty of ham, sausage, bacon—not a whole lot of beef because we didn't kill beef often. There was no refrigeration. Mama would can the sausage, and she'd take the ham and put them out in the smoke-house outside the house and cover them with salt, and they'd keep. Go out and cut it off and then soak it all night, so we could eat it the next morning.

It sounds good.

Oh, it was. We had no problem eating good food. No money. Didn't have any money, but we had plenty to eat.

And isn't that wonderful about those times, that people who were industrious enough and had a place to raise things could take care of themselves.

Right. Had a bunch of mules. And I had a horse. Never heard of a saddle. Didn't know what a saddle was. [Laughter] We rode bareback.

And what else did your dad raise on the farm?

We raised cotton, corn, peas, beans, potatoes. I know he'd have a big pile. They'd dig out a hole in the ground and a bank, fill it over with mud and stuff like that, you know, and go in there and put the sweet potatoes to keep during the winter. Ice potatoes he'd also put in there to keep during the winter. But then we'd—the peas, we'd shell them—and we had 60-gallon barrels, fill that up with crowder peas and apples and berries, stuff like that. Peanuts.

So it was a wealth of produce and fruit and—

Oh, yeah. We always had plenty. Back then we wore overhauls; I didn't have nothing but overhauls until I was fifteen years old.

Really. Well, you know, they're a great item of clothing. Comfortable, pockets, you can do things in them. So did he sell things at a market, or how did that work?

Sell cotton. When we were raising cotton after I got up a little—fourteen, fifteen years old and going to school — I would take the cotton to gin. And gin and bale the cotton is hard work, getting that gin, set the cotton up in there, you know. After I'd unload the cotton, get it ginned, the cottonseed would come out, and I'd put it in the wagon, unhitch the mules, water them, tie them to the wagon, and go to school.

Wow.

Then I'd come back after school. I'd smell good, you know, after doing all that. [Laughter] Then I'd come back after school, take the mules out and hitch them to the wagon, and go home, and load the wagon with another bale of cotton — we raised thirty or forty bales of cotton a year — to take the next day. But Daddy had people picking cotton and, of course, I had my turn, too, and it'd break my back, too. I hated that.

Children were a real asset to the family in those days. I mean you were a real contributing member of the family from the time you were very small.

Well, I was the oldest, and I had to help Daddy. I know Mama'd get up, and I don't know if you know what thickening gravy is or not, but she'd cook that white gravy, thickened gravy, and sausage, ham, and biscuits, and that was my breakfast. And sometime if we'd want eggs, we'd have them.

On Sunday morning sometimes, she'd fry chicken. In the morning. Especially if somebody had come—if people came they'd spend the night with you then because if they come they had to come in a wagon. Very few automobiles back in those days. But they'd spend the night, and Mama would always cook chicken. Young people, they'd wait until the grown people got through eating, and then they'd go in and eat what was left: not like it is today! [Laughter]

The balance has shifted, hasn't it? [Laughter]

The balance has shifted.

And so then as the other ones came along, they would have chores and be helping, too, but as the oldest, you had taken on the most responsibility.

Yes, because I was, as you can see here [pointing to list of his siblings and their birth dates], much older, and then I was gone. I left when I was seventeen, and, then, of course, they had chores, too. They had a lot of chores.

But of course things were more well-established by then. What about the boll weevil do you remember?

Oh, yeah, we had boll weevils, and Daddy had something he treated with for them. But he sold that cotton for four cents a pound. That was not much money.

How many pounds would a bale be?

I believe it's three or four hundred pounds.

Wow, that's a lot of work for that amount of money.

One-hundred twenty dollars. Yeah, a lot of work.

But the family was fed and sheltered.

Oh, yeah, yeah, and there was no heat in the house except what was in the fireplace. And no light except from the lamp.

CHAPTER 4

Four Miles in the Mud

So let's think about, say, when you were maybe ten or eleven years old and it's a school day. You do your chores and you have breakfast and then you go to school?

Yeah. Four miles. In the mud.

Four miles in the mud, right. And then when you got to school what was the situation? How many classes were there, how many children?

Well, the first one I attended was a little school right up the hill from the Camp home. First through seven in one room. That was where I went to the first grade. And everybody—the teacher taught the first, second, third, fourth through the seventh. I only went out there a year, but I remember it very well. Then I started at Dallas, six, I guess seven or eight years old. There'd be twenty, twenty-five students in a room.

And were they all grades then?

No. Separate grades. Dallas Elementary School.

I've heard people say who had been in one-room school houses—even though I know it was only that one year for you—that one nice part of it was that the younger children had the older children to kind of look up to and that there was a special sort of connection through the grades.

That's true.

And so then you went to the big school and then you were with just your own grade.

Right.

Were there any teachers or years that stood out to you?

Oh, yeah—Dr. Joe Matthews, his wife, Mrs. Irma Matthews—great teacher. I guess they felt sorry for me walking that far because the whole school started saving Blue Horse covers for me. You remember Blue Horse covers? It was a cover on the tablets. And I had 2,700 of them at the end of the year, and I had thirty-five cents to send those in, and I won a bicycle.

Really! So the school, the pupils, they did that for you.

They did that for me, and I started riding that bicycle to school, and I think I was probably twelve or thirteen years old. I'd ride it to school. For two years and some guy got on it one day and left it there, and he broke it.

Oh, but such a wonderful thing for everybody to participate and get you that bicycle. And Mrs. Matthews, she was your teacher for what grades or grade?

I think seventh, eighth, and ninth, I guess. Maybe sixth, seventh, eighth. I don't remember.

What subjects appealed to you when you were in school?

Math was easy. No problem. English was terrible. I had an awful time, but I had enough sense to take Latin. I passed it. But barely.

Well, but that's good for language.

I loved history. Loved history. But English was my toughest subject. Math was nothing and algebra—there was nothing to it. Even though I've forgotten—

I beg to differ. [Laughter] So, school days were basically happy—

Oh, yeah.

CHAPTER 5

Mama's Cooking

Did you bring lunch from home?

Yeah, I'd bring ham and biscuits or something like that. Mostly ham and biscuits, sausage and biscuits. And the Dallas crew lived in town—they'd want to give me a sandwich for my sausage biscuits.

I bet they did!

Instead of that loaf bread. [Laughter] And I did some of that; I'd swap them.

George's parents—Ida Evans Camp and William Maddox Camp—on their fiftieth anniversary.

It's fun to have the change, and lots of times it's easy to think the other person's is going to be better.

That's right.

So then you went home on school days, and you had more chores and homework.

Oh, yeah. When I got home I'd have to first get the wood for the fire-place, set it up on the porch. You better have that wood up there, or you'd freeze in the morning, and get the stove wood in. Then you go shuck a basket of corn to feed seven, eight, or nine mules because you didn't want to do that early in the morning. At 3:30 you wanted to have it ready to feed them. So I was pretty busy. I'd get home around four or four thirty, and it took me until around seven o'clock to get ready for bed. You went to bed as soon as you'd eat supper. Nothing else to do.

Right, it was dark.

It was dark, and then you went to bed, got warm. Instead of backing up against that open fire.

How many people did you have, sort of a dorm for the kids, did you share beds and keep warm that way?

Oh, yeah. My brother, Junior, and I slept together. You had to share a bed. Two double beds in a room. It was crowded.

Now every child has to have a room.

Oh, yeah. Their own bath.

But those experiences bring a lot in terms of relationships and just learning how to get along in narrow spaces.

Yes.

So then at night time you didn't have a big meal—probably you had supper?

Oh, no, we were hungry.

Oh, right. You'd been working all those hours.

I mean working. It wasn't walking around. It was manual labor.
Manual labor.

And so would you have—what kinds of things would you usually have for dinner?

Sometimes peas or beans or potatoes, always had potatoes and beans. Maybe some ham or something like that. A lot of times we didn't have any meat. Mostly vegetables. And plenty of it.

And I bet the vegetables were cooked with ham, too.

Yes. Always some kind of pie.

Oh, really.

Mama always had some kind of sweet.

You're making me hungry! [Laughter]

My Mama was a great, great cook. She cooked good!

Your son was talking about that, too. So you went to bed early. Now, in summertime things changed a little because you didn't have school. Right?

It changed. We'd eat breakfast about 4:30. After the mules would eat, then we'd go get them—the mules—put on the harness, water them. Go to the field and hitch them up, wait for daylight and start plowing. Plowed until about 11:30. And then we stopped for lunch, and we was back at the field. Plowed again from one until—that's in the spring of the year—until dark. And I know we had a lady that lived on that farm that had five boys. And I plowed with those boys. There was six of us.

Wow!

And, boy, we would get some work done. Prepare the land and get it ready for planting. Plant cotton and corn and beans and peas. Everything, peanuts, everything that you raised to eat. Because you had to eat. Didn't have the money to buy it—you had to raise it.

CHAPTER 6

One of the Smartest Men

But surely in the summer days there was some time that you just did other things?

Oh, yeah. When it was raining, you couldn't plow. There's work to do. You had to get your ax and go out there and clear off, get all the bushes coming up, to protect the crops so the crops would grow. There's always something to do on the farm. Every day there was no rest. No rest on a farm. You had to work. And my daddy believed in that and he, of course, he worked harder than we did. My daddy would take a drink when he got up in the morning, drink that white lightning.

Did he?

He'd take a drink, and he'd work all day, and he'd take a drink before he went to bed. [Laughter]

That's interesting.

That turned me against it. I've never been a drinking person.

But it didn't affect his productivity.

No.

But something about it, you just decided—

I hated it.

Why do you think you hated it?

I just didn't like it. I just didn't like him drinking it.

And so that just kind of affected you in that way.

But he and I were close. We were real close. And were—until he died.

How old were you when he died?

I was 65 years old.

Wow. You had him for a long time.

Yeah, he died when he was 90.

And he was healthy, like you are?

Oh, yeah. We'd walk in the woods and talk. He didn't have any education, but he was, I guess, one of the smartest men.

Where were the woods where you'd walk?

At his home.

Oh, so he stayed there. He was still on the farm.

Not on that one—he bought a farm later.

Let's talk a little bit about his background. How did he grow up; where did he grow up?

On that farm. He grew up there. On that same farm. His daddy died when he was young. He had one, two, three—let's see—Uncle Major, Uncle Nick, Uncle Johnny, and Uncle Watt. He had four brothers and a sister.

Yes.

Uncle Watt died young. Uncle Johnny lived to in his eighties. Uncle Major lived to his late eighties. And Aunt Liz lived to her nineties, the one sister. They all grew up on that farm.

Wow. And his only foray into the world other than farming was the time with Florida Power and Light in Miami?

Right.

Interesting.

And Mama wouldn't stay down there. She went through the hurricane, 1926.

CHAPTER 7

"Hold Your Own, Son"

You were about ten or eleven when the Great Depression hit. What were you aware of as a young boy in terms of what was going on?

Well, at that time, being raised on the farm, you didn't realize it was a hard time. I didn't know. All I knew is we got out and did what Daddy wanted to do.

Right.

And farm. Of course, we had this family with four boys. All of them but one older than me that worked on the farm. We were one of the largest farmers in the county at that time. And all I knew was work. And it didn't bother me. Never thought about it.

Right. And you didn't, there wasn't television reporting everything. You were—

No television. No radio. No electricity.

So you were just safe in your world that, where your parents provided for you—

That's right. All I thought about was the chores I had to do in the evening, getting in the wood and feeding the mules, getting the feed ready to feed them the next morning because we had six or seven mules to feed at that time. Daddy continued to farm pretty big like that until I left home; then he cut down. He continued to farm a little bit, but not like he did back in those days.

Right, right. The necessity days. Was there a place around where you grew up where you went swimming?

Yeah. In the creek. We called it a swimming hole; it was a creek someplace.

So you'd swim there in the summertime.

Swim there in the summertime.

Did you fish?

Yes. Fished. Fished a lot.

Where did you fish?

In Pumpkin Vine Creek, mostly in lakes. And we'd go in, and we'd catch 'em. I had a cousin that would go on the banks with his hand and he'd pull them out and he'd jump back and say, "Oh! There's a snake!" I'd never do that. I was afraid of that. Afraid of a snake. But he'd catch more fish with his hand than I'd catch with a pole. And we did a lot of seining.

Oh, a net.

We had a net, and we'd go down and pick them up.

I bet that was a nice change in terms of what you were eating.

We had an old telephone, one that you'd crank. You put that in the water and that would call the fish to jump up.

Really!

Some kind of, I don't know how that works. It would do something to the water. Crank that up and stir it up.

What kind of fish were they?

Mostly catfish.

That was fun, I bet.

Oh, yeah.

Do you remember as you grew up your family discussing politics or world events at all?

Oh, yeah. When I was a young fellow, my daddy—wasn't any politicians in Georgia, except Democrats. That's all we had. If you got elected in the primary, that was it. There was no such thing as a Republican back in those days. At least I didn't know any. They did discuss candidates. But as far as I knew I never heard any discussion other than about the candidates that were running, and they were all Democrats. No Republicans. If there were, I didn't know it.

Did some of them come out and shake hands and talk to your dad and mom?

Oh, yeah. Sheriff of the county, he'd always come by—because Daddy had people working for him and had the tenants on the farm. He wanted Daddy's support. They were the big politicians in the county. Didn't see any governors back in those days. Of course, Daddy used to go and see Gene Talmadge. I remember when I was a boy when Gene Talmadge would run, Daddy'd go to hear him talk.

Would they have an event, invite everybody?

Barbecue, yeah. I went one time with him. That's when I first met Herman. Herman's a little bit older than I was, but he and I got to know each other and continued to know each other.

Right, over the years.

Eugene Talmadge, political rally, July 4, 1942.
Lane Brothers Commercial Photographers Collection, Special Collections Department, Georgia State University Library.

Another thing of interest I happened to remember, I don't know, 1936, we had a fire at Cable Piano Company on Peachtree Street. I don't know whether you ever heard about that.

I did.

My cousin Terry Evans and his fiancée were burned up in it. My mama's brother's boy; he's my first cousin. His mother completely lost her mind, and his daddy lived to an old age, and never was the same. There's some bad things happened in my family, but the great majority of it's been good.

Of all the things that you learned from your parents, when you think back, what do you think was the most important or maybe long lasting?

Well, the best thing my parents taught me was to work and get the job done what I had to do, and I never will forget Daddy telling me, "Son, don't let those boys work harder and plow more ground than you do," he said. "Stay in there with them." [The four Mayfield boys]

Oh, those were the boys who worked with you—

Right. In the field, plowing and cutting corn, pulling fodder. But whatever we were doing, he said, "Hold your own, son; hold your own, son." He taught me that. He always said that. And I guess that's meant more to me than anything else. It taught me how to work and never back off from the chore that you had to do. Get it done.

CHAPTER 8

Never Missed a Party

Okay, parties. You were going to tell me about parties when you were a kid.

Yeah, when I was probably thirteen, fourteen years old. In the country, back in those days, on Saturday night somebody would have a party for the kids. Boys and girls, have a room in the house, you know, and you'd go to these parties, and they'd have somebody playing the guitar and the fiddle and dance and have a good time. I never missed one of those. Never missed one of those.

So the parents—they were providing some kind of entertainment for all the young people.

Oh, yeah. And as I got older, I started dreading to go to those because up in my neighborhood, up there, it was a pretty rough, a rough neighborhood, and it got to too much drinking, and my cousin and I and two other guys—I guess we were probably the only two boys in the county that didn't get out and drink a lot—we stayed together all the time. But a lot of fighting going on.

Really.

So when you say rough, these were all pretty much kids who were growing up the way you were. They were working hard and everything, so they just had excess energy that went off in negative ways?

Yeah, fighting over girls and stuff like that. [Laughter]

So then that started to be not be so much fun—

Yeah, drinking. Drinking's always been—well, its better now, but back in those days a lot of people made their living up in that part of the country, Paulding County, making moonshine.

Oh, so that's where the liquor came from.

That's right. You don't hear that anymore. Whiskey store's too close.

[Laughter]

So when you say dancing, what kind of dancing were you doing?

Square dancing.

So somebody called it.

Yeah.

Really, that does sound like fun.

That's all I knew.

And so there'd be some local people who liked to play and just bring their instruments.

Several people played the guitar and the violin and the piano. Hollering going on. [Laughter]

So there was some recreation available.

Yeah.

Clockwise from top: Ida and William Camp with grandchildren on their 50th wedding anniversary. Young George striding down a sidewalk in Atlanta. George with his parents and siblings

George's parents.

CHAPTER 9

Singing and Preaching

So during the day how much time did you have—your day really was taken up with the chores—

Oh, all my time.

So what about, say, family time or recreation? Sundays, did you work on Sunday too or did you take a day—

Of course, you had to feed the mules. And get the wood and stuff like that. You had chores on Sunday just like any other day, but you didn't get out and labor in the fields. We'd go over to church on Sunday. You had it once a month in those days where we went, and we'd go in a two-horse wagon. In the summertime they'd have dinner on the ground. You were talking about eating; oh, boy, good food! Everybody would bring food. But not in the wintertime.

And so it was once a month—it was maybe a preacher that traveled around to several churches.

Yeah. He had several churches. Four.

What kind of a service was it—what kind of church was it?

Baptist church.

And so there was preaching and singing.

Yes.

And was there—since they only met once a month—was there a young people's group? Or did they have anything special for the young people?

I didn't go to Sunday school in those days; if they had Sunday school I didn't know about it.

Well, I think you would have known about it. [Laughter]

Yes.

So then how did—you had your friends from school I guess. That's where you knew people your age.

Yeah, sad to think about that, with all of them gone. All of them gone, except me.

Really?

That I went to school with. The boys. There's a few girls left.

Speaking of girls. You had sisters, so you knew that girls and boys had sort of different outlooks about things maybe. How long were you in school?

Tenth grade. I did not graduate from high school. We had eleven grades then.

Oh, right, eleven. Yeah. Well, I think, too, in those days, that was a long time to make it because other things were calling you.

Yeah, I went into CCC camp in 1937, sent my check home for my Mama and Daddy. And the little ones. I only kept five dollars a month.

CHAPTER 10

Camp Applegate, Oregon

How did you hear about the CCC (Civilian Conservation Corps) camp? How did that come about?

Just a bunch of people around—my cousin joined, and some of my friends joined. And I just thought I could help Mama and Daddy out a little bit, and I went into the CCC.

And you were sixteen or seventeen?

Almost seventeen.

But you had to leave home.

I went to work in Oregon.

Oregon!

Rode a train a week out there, went through Needles, California. It's a train stop. And it was so hot, you couldn't breathe.

You said, "What have I done!"

What have I done? Of course, the train wasn't air conditioned, so it was hot on the train, too.

Camp Applegate. Camp Applegate in Oregon. I'll never forget that. Building roads. And for some reason, I was assigned kitchen detail. I never was out on the road. My responsibilities [were to] get up and prepare the kitchen for meals before and everything that goes on the table out there. Then during the day to clean it up and then do the same thing at lunch and dinner. So I did that all the six months I was there.

But on one occasion the warden came in and got me, told me he wanted me to take a trip with him. I didn't have any idea—of course, you did what the warden told you.

And the warden—that's what they called the person in charge of the camp?

[Nods to indicate yes.] We were checking fires, and we took off through the mountains. Up those mountains in Oregon—they're tough—trying to find fires.

Checking fires. Oh.

You just looked for fires. [We were] gone two days, slept in a bag at night.

How exciting.

We went in the woods. I didn't like that, I'm telling you, climbing over those mountains.

Well, you weren't used to it, weren't even used to the altitude, really.

That's right. It was terrible. I was glad to get back.

And so you were there for six months.

Yes.

And how did your family [take it]? You wrote back and forth, I suppose.

Got a letter once a month, something like that. Not much.

I bet they missed you after all those years.

Oh, yeah. It was hard on my mama and daddy.

CHAPTER 11

Learning How to Live

During the time when you heard about the opportunity represented by the CCC, I suppose you and other young people your age were thinking about what you might do to help out.

Oh, during that period of time all the young boys were going to the CCC camp because you didn't have no money back in those days. And there was an opportunity to make a little money. Most of my friends went to the CCC camp. I didn't stay but six months. I'd had enough of it.

Did some people stay longer? I don't know that much about the term of service. Would it be two years or could you leave when you wanted to?

Six months.

Oh, you signed up and then you would either re-up or not.

Thinking about that time—and I know there was that unpleasant experi-ence on the mountain—but when you look back, how does that time perhaps fit into how you began to formulate what seems to be a wonderful principle of how to manage people and that sort of thing.

Well, I didn't have any management experience then. I always worked in the kitchen except that one trip.

But you were learning because you were at the bottom—

Right. At the bottom. But that didn't help me much. Not until I got out and come back home. What helped me I guess more than anything to establish a foundation was when I went to work for an insurance company.

And that's when you started to see what was good and what wasn't in terms of—

Oh, yes.

Talk about that—

That day—I'll never forget that. We had been bird hunting, and we were standing on the side of a dirt road and George Sheffield was getting ready to get in his car and come back to Atlanta. His dad was treasurer of the Life Insurance Company of Georgia. And his daddy was also one of the starters of the Life of Georgia. But I couldn't believe he wanted me to go to work. Didn't know where I was going or what I was going to do. [Laughter]

Right. So then, again, you were working for other people but you probably started to observe how people did things and maybe—

I was handling my [accounts] and billing and selling insurance, managing, and I had $22.50 a week to live on. And had a car and I was coming home on weekends to see Martha. That's the best thing that ever happened to me: Martha.

You mentioned being a Mason, being in the Masonic group and I'm just wondering, how did you become interested in that?

I had got to know a few people in the Masonic order. Nobody ever asked me to join. I decided I wanted to become a Mason. And I think that helped me more at that stage in my life than anything else probably. Outside of my home life, one of the best things I ever done.

It was the people that you met and the way things were done or what was it?

Oh, I can't go into detail.

Okay.

I learned how to live.

You did—

I learned how to live. And I'll never regret that. Great thing for me.

And it was something that you saw from the outside and were drawn to—so that's interesting. Maybe on some level you knew you needed something.

I needed what they had. People that I knew, but nobody ever asked me. They don't ask you; you had to apply and hope you were accepted. You were investigated pretty thoroughly before you were accepted.

You've been involved in a lot of investigations. [Laughter]

That's the name of my game! [Laughter]

Certificate of Discharge

from

Civilian Conservation Corps

HONORABLE

TO ALL WHOM IT MAY CONCERN:

THIS IS TO CERTIFY THAT * GEORGE W. CAMP CC4-276866 A MEMBER OF THE

CIVILIAN CONSERVATION CORPS, WHO WAS ENROLLED April 16, 1938 AT
(Date)

Ft. McPherson, Georgia. IS HEREBY DISCHARGED THEREFROM, BY REASON

OF ** "Expiration term of enrollment for the convenience of the U.S."

SAID George W. Camp WAS BORN IN Dallas,

IN THE STATE OF Georgia ' WHEN ENROLLED HE WAS 17 YEARS

OF AGE AND BY OCCUPATION A Truck Driver HE HAD Brown EYES,

Brown HAIR, Ruddy COMPLEXION, AND WAS 6 FEET

INCHES IN HEIGHT. HIS COLOR WAS White

GIVEN UNDER MY HAND AT Fort McPherson, Ga. THIS 30th DAY

OF September , ONE THOUSAND NINE HUNDRED AND Thirty-Eight

(Name) (Title)

Comdg. CCC Conditioning Camp

C. C. C. Form No. 2
April 5, 1933

*Insert name, as "John J. Doe".
**Give reason for discharge.

2—10171

CHAPTER 12

Getting out of the Country

So you were there at the CCC camp for about six months and then what happened? Let's clarify the story of how you got started into your professional life.

We're moving, getting away from a lot of stuff here, but I came home and started to work on the farm. And I hunted a lot in those days. When I was little, about seven years old, Daddy bought me a single-barrel shotgun. Ronnie has it now.

Oh, really.

And I had a bunch of beagles, and I'd rabbit hunt. And you'd kill those rabbits and take them to Dallas to sell them. I'd get three gun shells for a rabbit or fifteen cents. I continued to do that, and I got to hunting a lot, but George Sheffield—you've heard of Life Insurance Company of Georgia—his daddy and two other men started the Life Insurance Company of Georgia. And George was the secretary at that time. And I'd go bird hunting with him on Saturdays. George was probably fifteen to twenty years older than I was. One Saturday we'd come in; we'd been bird hunting. I'd kill birds back then. I could shoot them and kill them. That's one of the reasons he liked to hunt with me, I guess. He asked me when we come back to the car, and he said, "When you going to work?"

I said, "I am working."

He said, "You know, you got to go get a job and go to work."

I said, "I got a job. I'm working with my daddy."

"No, that's not what I mean. I'm going to get you out of the country."

I said, "What do you want me to do?"

He said, "I want you to be in Birmingham two weeks from Monday and report to Mr. Miller, 710 Woodward Building, and tell him I sent you over there."

I said, "Okay, I'll do that."

So he saw potential in you.

Well, I didn't know how I was going to get there. I didn't have any money. So I went up to the bank, First National Bank. Mr. Bird was president of the First National Bank of Dallas. And Billy Bird was in my class. (Billy went on to become a Methodist preacher, in Georgia. He retired and died about three months ago.)

I told Mr. Bird, "What am I going to do? I've got to have some money." I wanted to borrow some.

He said, "How much you need?"

I said, "I think I can get by on twenty dollars."

He reached in the drawer, pulled out twenty dollars and handed them to me. Took me six months to pay that twenty dollars back.

And how far did it go? What did that twenty dollars buy you then?

Well, I caught a bus, went to Birmingham, found a boarding house. Cost me five dollars a week.

For room and board?

For room and board, three meals a day. I went up to that office on Monday morning and asked for Mr. Miller. He come out and said, "Who are you?"

I told him, and he said, "What you doing here?"

I said, "Mr. George Sheffield sent me here."

"What do you mean?"

Oh, no!

And so he said, "Wait a minute." He went in there. I don't know what he said to George. All of a sudden he started saying, "Yes, sir; yes, sir; yes, sir." He came back out, and I started selling life insurance. Gave me a little folder—I've still got it. I went out, and didn't have nothing, and [they] started paying me $22.50 a week, and I thought I was rich.

Oh, I bet—

Thought I was rich. But that was, I was a little over seventeen years old.

You'd lived on the farm and you'd been up there at the CCC, and, of course, you'd been to church, but other than that, it was new to you, even what to wear, (not to mention having the clothes) and how to approach people and what to do. They just threw you in the water.

I'll never forget. I'd never had cereal in my life. The first morning at the boarding house, they came out with cereal, I didn't know what it was. Never had seen cereal before. [Laughter]

Breakfast? Where are the biscuits?

That's the way it was.

So did you watch the other people and see that they put milk in it?

Well, that's what I did. [Laughter] That's exactly right. That's exactly what I did.

Oh, my goodness, that's a great story.

George and Martha on their wedding day.

CHAPTER 13

After That Day, That Was It

Let's talk a little more specifically about when you and Martha got married.

Well, I tell you, there was two good-looking girls in the county up there, Martha Wigley and Marjean Grogan. I was dating Marjean, and Dennis Gunnell asked me one day to take him down to see Ruth Wigley (that's Martha's sister) Sunday afternoon. I had a convertible, '32 Ford convertible. So I took him down there. Down to her house. A farm about four miles from ours. And that started it. And when I was in Birmingham, I'd come home on weekends to see her. And I did that for two years.

I'd known Martha off and on—all my life, actually—but I'd never thought about dating her. I knew she was a beautiful girl, but after that day, that was it. I never went back to see Marjean anymore.

All of a sudden, you knew right away.

Yeah. We dated four years. That was the latter part of 1937. And dated four years before we got married. That's one of the best things that ever happened to me.

Do you remember your proposal?

Yeah.

Care to share it?

She and I had discussed it awhile and decided we would; three weeks after we discussed it, three weeks, we got married. Preacher Smith came down. Martha was living with her sister at that time out on Cascade Road in Cascade Heights. And he came down and my parents came down and her parents came down. We were married in her sister's home. And got on a train and went to Birmingham. Take two days, come back, went to work.

We were married six months when the army called me back in. And then I stayed almost four years in the army.

I know you say that marrying Martha was the best thing that ever happened to you. Let's have a little more of a description of her as a person.

Well, Martha, is, she is a good housekeeper; she looked after me. And the best mother. She looked after the boys. I don't know whether we have enough time for me to say enough good things about her. She did a great job. And there's a bunch of girls from her family, but I got the best one. Good cook, fed me well. The only problem that I ever had with her—she didn't know it; I never told her. I'd be gone a week somewhere, out working, and I'd come home Friday night, and she wanted to go out to eat.

She'd been alone all week; you'd been out eating all week. [Laughter] *So you had to work that out.*

I went with her. I never said no. Never said no.

That was the right thing to do. And nice.

Oh, yeah. But I've been real lucky. Oh, we've had our differences from time to time, minor, nothing major. Nothing major. Nothing major. Both been pretty healthy up until now. But I have no complaints. I wouldn't change a thing if I had it to do over again.

Oh, that's great—that's wonderful.

How did you find out that you were going to be a parent for the first time? Do you remember how she told you about that?

It wasn't her. The doctor told me; it was when he told me, Dr. Fisher. Crawford Long Hospital.

Thinking back to when your children were little, were there some things that either amazed you or maybe the funniest thing one or the other of them did or said as a small child.

Well, I had two characters; they were good boys. They were good boys. One time Martha called me and she says, "I'm next door, I can't get in the house."

And I said, "What's the matter?"

She said, "Ronnie locked me out."

He was a little bitty thing, but some way he locked the door. I had to go home and open the door. He was in there by himself, in the house. [Laughter] I'll never forget that. She was upset about that.

Right, that's a scary thing to have a little child in the house alone. What did you find most difficult about raising children or their childhood years?

Well, I didn't believe in ever turning them loose. I never turned my boys loose; I played with them all the time, you know, and tried to keep up with what they're doing, when and where they were going and I'd tell them when I wanted them to be home. Most of the time they'd come home. A lot of times Ronnie wouldn't. He'd get carried away enjoying himself. That always upset me. I couldn't go to sleep until he come home. But I worried about them; I worried about them. I was lucky. If they'd got in any bad trouble, I didn't know about it. They'd keep it from me. But I had real good boys, and when they went to college, they never knew when I was going to drop by.

Oh, really.

When they were older, I'd call them in the morning and get them out of bed. They didn't like that. I'd enjoy getting them on the phone, early in the morning and talk to them. They didn't like that, but I'd still call them. They knew I was around and that I was their dad, and I didn't believe in turning them loose until they finished college. And I have no complaints. Like I say I wouldn't be here long enough to tell you how proud I am of them both. They've made a good living; they're good family persons.

That's wonderful.

I'm a lucky man.

I was going to ask you what you found most rewarding about being a parent, but I think you've already answered that. I guess, too, it's nice; you had the phase when they were little and the variety of things that happened as they were growing up, but now that they're settled and have their own families, there are new rewards.

That's right. That's right.

You know, Ronnie lives right down there. [Pointing towards the backyard]

Really? Right over there? So can you walk through here or—oh, yeah! Oh, that's great!

Two blocks, down the street. Alan lives two miles, a mile and a half this way. [Gesturing]

Now you are lucky in that.

I've been real lucky.

My grandchildren born and raised and lived up right around here. You never knew when you were going to look up and see one of them walking in.

Oh, I bet you love that, too.

Oh, yeah. Once they become a teenager and get out of high school, they get busy. You don't see a lot of them then.

Oh, you are blessed.

I know I'm blessed; I am really blessed.

CHAPTER 14

Mama and Daddy at the Bell Bomber Plant

Tell a little more about when your family was farming on a large scale in Paulding County.

I remember picking cotton, pulling fodder and gathering stuff and hauling corn and putting it in the barn. We raised 1,500 bushels of corn and fifty or sixty bales of cotton [a year]. And hay, I hated that job because I'm allergic, and it would sting and I'd almost go crazy.

But allergy wasn't a reason not to do it, huh?

That's right. But after I left home, my daddy farmed two years—of course, at that time when World War II started, he went to work for Bell Bomber in Marietta (Lockheed).

Really.

Yeah. He and my mother both. In 1941.

So in 1941 your father and mother both went to work.

It could have been '42. At Bell Bomber in Marietta (Lockheed). They were building B-29's.

Now what's the distance? Did they still get to stay at home?

Oh, yeah, they stayed at home.

It's not right there, is it?

It's about twelve miles.

How did they get there? Did they have a car?

They had a car.

I wonder what that commute was like.

Oh, well, they had built Highway 41 during the war, you know. That made it easier to get to the plant. There was a few paved roads, but not around their house—still mud then.

Who's Afraid of the Big Bad Shortage, 38-0 Wants to Know

Ida Camp, assembler in Dept. 38-0, was honored last week by fellow workers at a surprise birthday luncheon, which featured — shortages notwithstanding — fried chicken, country ham and sausages, assorted sandwiches and salads, and "all kinds of cakes."

Chairman of arrangements for the luncheon was Ethel Hughes, and she was assisted by Grace Hardy, Avie Allen and Eva Edwards.

The honoree received a number of gifts, among which was a large decorated birthday cake, topped with candles. Coffee and soft drinks were served with the luncheon.

"It would have been perfect," said Mrs. Camp, "if my serviceman son could only have been here." Sgt. G. W. Camp, stationed at Newport News, Va., has visited Bell several times. "He thinks we're doing a splendid job," his mother continued, "and says he hopes I'll keep buying bonds and building bombers until he comes home."

Comments from George's mother appeared in *The Bell Bomber News.*

So they had these jobs, but what happened to all the farm work with them gone working?

They had a garden. That's all; they had a big garden.

So all the children—

They were all in school. Of course, they had their chores, too. Not as much as my brother and I did because there wasn't as much going on. My mother and daddy worked awful hard raising us. There was a lot of us.

Now what were they doing at the plant—working on assembly lines?

The lines, yeah. I think Daddy was a carpenter building something, crates or whatever. I don't know exactly what my mother did. I know I went over there one time and toured the plant with Daddy. And I was in service at that time; I was home on leave. And I went through the B-29, went through that.

Did you wear your uniform?

Oh, yeah. I wore my uniform. I was a sergeant when I came home.

I bet he enjoyed walking around the plant with you that day.

Uh, huh.

CHAPTER 15

You're in the Army Now

I joined the army, April 8th, 1941.

So it was in the air then, all the young men were feeling the—

Right. I was sending my parents a fifty-dollar check a month. You did that in the army. And looked like—Japanese hadn't yet gone and bombed Pearl Harbor, and it looked like everything had quieted down some. I got out on reserves, and I went back and found a boarding place on Gordon Street in Atlanta, in the West End area, which was the best community in Georgia at that time. And moved in there, in this boarding house, and when the guys who lived there came home one night I met them. One of them, Jake, asked me what I was going to do. I said, "I don't know. I'm going to try to find out tomorrow."

He said, "Just stay here until tomorrow night."

I said, "What do you mean?"

He said, "I think I've got a job for you."

He came back the next day and said, "You've got a job with me."

Let me go back to when I went in the army the first time. I was assigned to the machine records unit, which was the beginning of data centers, just like this. [Gesturing to indicate his son Ron's company, where this session took place.]

Really! Isn't that something!

I didn't know why in the world I was assigned to that data center. But I found out later. I made 137 on the test I took, out of a possible 150. Lots of people never made over 120. So they put me in the data center; nobody knew anything about IBM in those days and all that stuff.

It was your math and your—

I never had no problem with math.

Your jobs found you, didn't they?

Yes. When he came home, Jake said, "You got a job. Just go to work with me tomorrow."

And where was the job?

Candler Warehouse. West End.

And what did you do there?

Operated a 305 tabulating machine, sorters, all IBM equipment.

At this time, Martha lived with her sister on Cascade Road, about two miles from where I was. I did not have a car then, but I was making $105 a month—$105 a month. A lot of money. So at the end of 1941, we decided we were going to get married. And we did, on February the 21st, 1942. Had a nice little apartment.

Where was that?

On Hopkins Street, in West End. We were comfortable and happy.

When Pearl Harbor hit—we'd already decided to get married when Pearl Harbor hit. The lady I was boarding with woke me up that morning, telling me war had started, told me about Pearl Harbor, and I turned on the radio. Scared me to death. But that's why I don't drive Japanese cars today. Don't want a Japanese car in my driveway.

Oh, really.

Cost me four years of my life.

So you had already decided to get married, then Pearl Harbor, and then you got married.

We were married six months, and I was called back to active duty. Went to Fort Benning. Stayed there until the early part of '43. And we were in—what we did then was to assign troops all over the country, army troops, and then we broke out the air force when I was there, and the air force started their own machine-records unit. Then we went to Hampton Road Point of Debarkation, and I thought I was going overseas. But we settled there. And they wouldn't let me go. I stayed there and after embarkation, I was in charge of one shift at that time. We operated seven days a week, twenty-four hours a day, preparing passenger lists to go overseas, put on the ship, and ship to wherever they were going.

I hadn't been there too long until I became the NCO in charge of the unit. I reported to the captain. I was a young kid, twenty-three years old, and I had forty to fifty civilians and a couple hundred soldiers working for me there. And once I got that I asked Martha, and she moved up there.

Oh, so you didn't have to be apart. That was good.

I stayed there all during the war.

Did you want to go overseas?

Yes, I did. Half of my unit went. I left something out. Before I got to

Hampton Road I applied for and was accepted to go to OCS. Officer's
Candidate's School.

I would imagine you would be—

Ordnance, in Aberdeen, Maryland. I went there, and I'd been there—I
think it was thirteen weeks—and I finished ten weeks of it, and I was on
a twenty-five-mile hike with full field equipment and got gassed in the
river.

No!

They did it on purpose, training purposes. And on [the way] back I fell
out.

You mean they did that with real gas, training?

Training, yeah. Not bad.

It sounds terrible.

My leg gave out on me, my left leg. They never told me. Just told me
that I wasn't physically able to be an officer. And I didn't find out until
I got out of the army. And my mama told me when I was two or three
years old, I had a terrible sickness. And Julian Johnson, my doctor for a
lot of years, told me I had polio—because my left leg is smaller than my
right leg.

Really. And so that was what caused that weakness that made you not—

Right. And that's why I didn't make it. Everything else was all right. But then I stayed there until January the 14th, 1946. Found a lady out there that had a little 1937 Plymouth. I bought it. Three hundred dollars. And got some tires. Martha and I loaded that thing up, headed to Georgia.

That's when I got out. Rode down to her sisters and no place to stay. No furniture. Just what we had in that car. Nothing. But, in the meantime, I'd been sending her an allowance. I was able to send her fifty dollars a month and Mama and Daddy fifty dollars a month. But Martha never spent a dime of her money. That story will come later, but not a dime did she spend of that money. She put it all in the bank.

Well, that was great.

Gordon Street in West End, looking west, 1952.
Tracy O'Neal Photographic Collection, Special Collections Department, Georgia State University Library.

CHAPTER 16

George Camp, Prophet

After we got to her house, I went to Fort McPherson two or three days and got discharged. I went back to Candler Warehouse; they wanted me to come to work. I'd been promoted while I was gone because that was the law then—I was up to about two thousand a year. And I was planning to go back there and go to work at Candler Warehouse.

In the meantime, I had to find a place to live. Well, I got to knocking on doors. West End, go down the street knocking on doors. Couldn't find anything. Found this lady, elderly lady.

[Pause]

So you are back from the service, and you are looking for a place to live.

Yeah, I met this lady. She came to the door, and she said, "I've got an apartment, but I think I've decided who I'm going to rent it to." Oh, I twisted her arm—I talked to her. [Laughter] And I got it! It was a little three-bedroom apartment in the back of her house. Her husband was an engineer with the railroad. Mr. and Mrs. Carol. I really enjoyed living there, and we lived there in that apartment four years. And we bought a lot. Bought a new car. Then we built our house and moved.

So how long did you live there?

Four years. And Ronnie was born there. We moved two weeks after he was born.

Getting back to where I went to work, Candler Warehouse. They had a machine-records unit here in Atlanta, which is the same thing that I worked at the Hampton Road Point of Embarkation.

A machine—

A machine-records unit. We know it today as a data center. Same thing. They called me. Since I came home and I'd been doing that for four years in the army, they called me and offered me a job level seven at a salary of forty-eight-ninety-seven-twenty.

Wow!

That was a big job in 1946. But I had three hundred military and two hundred civilians working for me.

Oh, my gosh, you still were pretty young—

Twenty-six years old. Made me sick to cut orders.

Really, just the worry of—

Yeah. And all these soldiers were trying to get out of the army, go home. But I got through it and had a good doctor and got through it.

Let's talk a little bit about how you looked at the job and how you were able to manage that many people.

Well, I learned to manage in the army. The army taught me management. Taught me how to handle people. The army knows how to handle people.

That's true.

I didn't hesitate. If something went wrong, I corrected it. Man, woman, or child, it didn't bother me, and I went home. But I always tried to do the right thing. I didn't like hurting people. You know, tried to do the right thing, and I explained to them why I did what. I always did that.

Was there already a certain hierarchy of management or did you establish one? How did that work?

No, there was a colonel in charge of it. He was a guy—the colonel in charge—was a guy that I went in the army with, as a private.

Really—

Yeah. He went to OCS, and he and I were friends, but he was not the one that called me. Somebody else called me to come up there. But then they had an administrative assistant, a man that was an administrative assistant, and he had an assistant, which was a lady. And they are the ones I reported to. I stayed there, and then that office was located behind the old post office building in downtown Atlanta.

In 1947, a year later, they wanted to move the machine-records unit to Fort McPherson, get away with paying that rent. But before we went out there—this is interesting, I don't know whether you remember this or not—we was going to have a railroad strike in this country, and the president was going to stop that. I don't remember too much about it other than the fact that we went through and pulled all the transportation people with all these punch cards that we had to get the qualified people to take over the railroad if the president, Harry Truman, decided to break that strike. I know I worked on that two weeks, getting that ready for him. But we didn't call them because the strike was settled. He was ready to handle that.

Colonel Warden was the adjunct general in charge of the Third Army. He come up here and Fred Hastert, who was the lieutenant colonel in charge of MRU, he transferred somewhere else and Colonel Warden and I came up with a plan for a new building to house a machine-records-unit (what we know today as a data center) for Fort McPherson. The contractor built it, and we moved out there the latter part of 1947. Moved our office out there.

And that was just two miles from my house. I worked there until 1955. Ronnie was born April 17th, 1950. And one of the things that always amused me, and I don't know how in the world this happened. Gwendolyn Fields, one of the women that worked for me, her and the girls, we had a bunch of girls, always giving me a rough time, kidding, and one day Gwendolyn asked me—we were having lunch, like you and I did today—and she said, "When is Martha expecting?"

I said, "She's going to the hospital on April the 17th , at four o'clock in the morning."

And when was this that you said that?

It was two or three months before he was born. And it went just that way. He was born at four o'clock in the morning on April 17th.

Now how do you think that happened?

I don't know! [Laughter] All those girls and Martha sure gave me a hard time after that!

I bet they did. They thought you were a prophet. [Laughter]

That actually happened.

CHAPTER 17

"You're Going to Take It"

In 1947 I went into the Masonic Order. And I was kind of active in catechism and the commanding general, not the commanding, deputy general, deputy commanding general, Third Army, was President Harry Truman's first cousin, General Truman. You might have read about him here in Atlanta. When he retired he went to work for the state. He joined the Masonic Order. And when he did, he would come over at lunch time and get in an office and get me in there to teach him the catechism.

And this lieutenant colonel in charge, he never said nothing to me about it. He was my boss out there, but he never said nothing to me about it. I didn't think about him not liking it. But he was a Catholic and I've never been one to—a Catholic, Jew, Protestant, makes no difference to me. I respect all of them. But, anyway, he didn't say a word until General Truman was transferred in 1954; he started giving me a hard time. And one day he came out there and started to give me a hard time. I told him, I said, "You need to go slap to hell! You can have this job!"

And the reason I said that, J. W. Bullock, who was in charge of State Farm, had been trying to get me, for two years, to become a State Farm agent. And he happened to be there that day; I told him I just resigned. He said, "You ready to go to work?" [Laughter] On Monday morning I was a State Farm agent.

You'd moved on to your next job.

I went up there, and I worked one year. I worked with Don Fowler, he and I worked for J. W. Bullock on Gordon Street. We were new agents. He started paying me a hundred dollars a week. I wasn't earning that because I didn't have any business, but they'd give you a hundred dollars until you built up your business. I stayed there a year, about a year. Ronnie was small, and Alan was a baby, and I was working long hours. I'd get up early, and I'd stay out until nine, ten o'clock, as long as I was talking to people. And doing all right, doing well.

When I went home one night, and I knew as soon as I went into the house that something was wrong. I said to Martha, "What's the matter?"

"The post office," she said, "wants to see you."

"For what?" I asked.

"The controller of the postal service wants to talk to you."

"How do you know that?"

"He called me," she said, "and I told him you'd be down there." [Laughter]

I said, "You should not have told him that."

She said, "You're going."

I said, "What do you want me to do that for? I'm happy."

"I'm tired," she said, "of you being gone all the time."

"All right," I said, "I'll go and see him."

So I went down there and talked to the controller. And I didn't know at that time that the post office was as political as it was. (This was during the Eisenhower administration.) Well, I was born and raised a Democrat. That's all there was in my day in Georgia: a Democrat. Didn't know nothing else. They asked me what I was. I said, "I'm a Georgia boy." Then I asked him, "Why did you call me?"

He said, "IBM recommended we call you. We need somebody to take over a shift in the data center here."

I said, "Well, I'll have to think about that."

He said, "Will you let us know tomorrow?"

Even though you'd told them your party affiliation?

Yes. "I'll have to go home and talk to my wife. I'll call you tomorrow," I said. I went home and told Martha, and she said, "You're going to take it." [Laughter]

That would be a nicer day-to-day life for her.

So I called them, and I still didn't know about politics, and they hired me, on the phone. I give J. W. notice, State Farm, and quit.

And I went up there and went to work—it was a shift—and there was resentment. People, a lot of people there, every one of them thought they ought to have the job. I understood that, and it didn't bother me. But it wasn't easy to go in there new, but even though I'd been in it for twenty years, and I knew what I was doing, it wasn't easy to go in there. It took a little while.

I'd been there two or three weeks and a guy eased up to me one day, and he says, "Who's your sponsor?"

I said, "My what?"

"Your sponsor."

I said, "What are you talking about?"

He says, "Who endorsed you?"

I said, "Well, what do you mean endorsed me?"

He said, "Come on, some politician put you in here."

I said, "No politician put me in here." I never heard of such a thing. And he didn't believe me that I didn't have a sponsor. Well, I didn't. I hadn't been there very long. I was in charge of one shift of the data center.

How many shifts did they work, three?

Three, and I had one. I had the day shift because I wouldn't take the second or third shift. I told them. They sought me—I didn't seek the job.

And somebody at home was voting.

Yeah. And the guy, his name was Birch; I forget his first name. One day he came in and resigned. I never knew why; he and his wife moved back to Texas. I don't know why he resigned. And I didn't know what to do. I just went on with my job, minding my own business. And two weeks later I got a call from the controller to come in there, and he give me the job. Ten thousand dollars a year.

Goodness!

241P EST MAY 26 64 AH198
IC211 WC271 WW SNB046 GOVT PD SN WASHINGTON DC 26 112P EDT
ON GEORGE W CAMP, ACTING POSTMASTER
 ATLA
M PLEASED TO ADVISE SENATE HAS JUST CONFIRMED YOUR NOMINATION
O BE POSTMASTER. REGARDS.
 DICK RUSSELL
28).

1030A EST MAY 27 64 AF092
RA143 WD080 WW SNA019 GOVT PD SN WASHINGTON DC 27 1045A EDT
HON GEORGE W CAMP
 POSTMASTER ATLA
HAPPY TO INFORM YOU SENATE HAS CONFIRMED YOUR APPOINTMENT AS
POSTMASTER
 HERMAN E TALMADGE
 (49).

TELEGRAM

449P EST JUN 19 64 AH429
 A LLT169 PD FAX ATLANTA GA 19 428P EST
HON GEORGE CAMP, ATLANTA POSTMASTER
 MAIN POST OFFICE FORSYTH ST ATLA
DEAR GEORGE: DUE TO A HEAVY SCHEDULE I WAS UNABLE TO ATTEND
YOUR CEREMONIES THIS AFTERNOON. MAY I EXTEND TO YOU MY BEST
WISHES FOR A LONG AND CONTINUED SUCCESSFUL CAREER
 CARL E SANDERS GOVERNOR
 (46).

TELEGRAM

1147A EST AUG 16 63 AH133
 A LLC110 PD ATLANTA GA 16 1131A EST
GEORGE W CAMP, DLR 1245PM AUG 17, NEW POSTMASTER POST OFFICE
 FEDERAL COURT RM 322 MAIN POST OFFICE BLDG ATLA
HEARTIEST CONGRATULATIONS ON YOUR APPOINTMENT REST ASSURED
OF THE CITIES COOPERATION IN CARRYING OUT THE FINE POSTAL SERVICE
WHICH WE KNOW YOU WILL CONTINUE TO PROVIDE WITH BEST WISHES
I AM SINCERELY
 IVAN ALLEN JR MAYOR OF ATLANTA
 (45).

Telegrams from Senator Richard Russell, Senator Herman Talmadge, Governor Carl Sanders, and Mayor Ivan Allen.

CHAPTER 18

The New Kid on the Block

I thought I'd arrived. I wasn't expecting to get it because I was the new kid on the block. I wasn't expecting to get it. I worked hard. And I was fully qualified because I'd been in that over twenty years at that time. It was 1956 when, I guess, I got that job. A year or so later, Mr. Lawrence—I had three men in my life that meant a lot to me; he was one of them—called me down to the office. He was the type of man that'd just call you in and just chew you out. Just cuss you out. He did that to me several times. But always something good come out of it. I never—I'd just sit there and listen, you know. He called me and said, "George."

"Yes, sir," I said.

"I want you to be postmaster," he said.

"Postmaster, for what?"

"Postmaster of Atlanta," he said.

"Why do you want me to be postmaster?"

"Earl Sanders is retiring," he said.

And actually, I don't know whether they pushed him out—I don't know. I don't know what happened. But he retired. So I said to Mr. Lawrence, "Well, are you going to give it to me?"

And when I said that, boy, he jumped up. He raised cane. And I was just as sincere as I could be—I didn't know. I've been dumb a lot of times in my life. But he said, "No. Don't you know how you get that? Congressmen and senators appoint you. You know so-and-so, naming a congressman whose name I've forgotten.

"I've met them," I said. I knew some politicians because of Daddy, but I'd never been politically active in my life. I knew Senator Russell. Greatest senator that ever lived, I think. And Senator Talmadge. I knew Senator Talmadge all my life. But there was this congressman out there that lives in Stone Mountain, somewhere out in there, I forget his name, and Mr. Lawrence told me to call him. And I said, "What am I going to say to him? I don't know him."

"You call him," he said.

I called. He wouldn't talk to me.

That's like walking into that job in Alabama.

That's right. He said Charlie Weltner was running for Congress. And he was running against the county unit system, when you had so many votes per county in the state of Georgia. I don't know if you remember the county unit system or not.

I've read about that, yes.

So Charlie Weltner was a friend of mine. He was in politics for a little while, and he died five or six years ago, was chairman of the Supreme Court of Georgia when he died. And I got involved, meeting Charlie, raising money for him, working for him. We got him elected. He beat the other guy, and he went to Congress. And this postmaster position, he asked me several times, "You want it?"

"I don't know whether I do or not, Charlie." I was afraid of it, to be honest with you; I was just afraid of the job. And he asked me why I was afraid of it. I said, "Well, the black and white situation, what is going on now. I don't believe in giving anybody preferential treatment. Do what's right. Be fair. Promote on merit."

It went on like that for three or four months. One morning—I got to work about seven, seven fifteen. Senator Russell called me at seven thirty in the morning, and he said, "George, how come you haven't taken that job?"

I said, "What job, Senator?"

"The postmaster."

"I'm afraid of it," I said. (At that time there were no women at the post office except in secretarial jobs. There was only one black supervisor.) Then he asked, "How do you operate?"

I said, "I believe in operating on merit, promoting on merit."

We talked about thirty minutes, and he said, "George, if I told you nobody would bother you, would you take that job?"

I said, "Who's going to keep them from bothering me?"

"I am," he said.

"Well," I said, "I'll take it under those conditions." And I hung up.

I didn't think any more about it. That was between 7:30 and 8:00 o'clock that morning. About ten o'clock I saw Charlie Weltner's assistant walking up and down that hall and going up to the regional director's office. He wasn't talking to me. I didn't know nothing. The paper come out at 11:30; my name was in headlines: the Atlanta Postmaster. Nobody called and told me nothing.

That was just it—in that conversation.

George, Martha, Alan, and Ronnie with W.W. McMillon on August 17th, 1963.

That was it. So of course a lot of people in there—political hacks, as I call them but I shouldn't call them that—they resented it [that I got the position]. They didn't like it. Newcomer. New kid on the block. But then I was sworn in the next Saturday, as acting postmaster. It was August the 17th, I think, 1963. And I didn't get confirmed that year. The Senate didn't confirm me until the next spring. I was acting for about a year because the United States Senate had to confirm me.

I've been before the Senate committee several times in my time. Once I was confirmed, Senator Russell sent me a letter notifying me. And had a big party—Millsby Lane, who got to be a good friend, gave me a big party.

Oh, isn't that nice!

All the Atlanta elite was there; I met all the leadership back then, Ivan Allen, Judge Griffin Bell, his office was right over mine. We'd have coffee every morning. I was real lucky. Associated with all the leadership in the state actually. Carl Sanders, I liked him; Carl's a good friend, gave the best advice, other than Gus Lawrence, who was the guy who got me all the way up there. The next man was Senator Dick Russell, greatest human being I ever knew, other than my daddy, I guess. He'd always said, "Son, you always put your country first on anything you do." Never heard a politician say that before him.

I don't know that it's said very often now.

No, we don't have nothing like that no more. I used to go to dinner with him and Margaret Chase Smith. They kind of dated—you know, she was a senator from Maine—and the Republican senator, Howard Baker's father-in-law—I forget his name, but the three of them, and me. I did dinner with them. I did that quite often. And this Republican senator and Russell they'd fight and argue. Once they'd reach a decision they'd shake hands—Everett Dirksen, that's who it was, great man—they'd ask each other, is that best for the country? And they'd shake hands. And that's the way it'd go. We don't have that kind of leadership in Washington anymore.

But when I went to Washington, which I did quite often, I always went to Senator Russell's office. I didn't care who was in his office—they'd come out, I went in. He was awful good to me, Senator Russell was— great man, great man. For me and my family he did so much—he doesn't realize what he did. I know when Dick Nixon was elected president I went in, I called him about 7:30 in the morning. I said, "Well, Senator Russell, there's going to be an ass beating."

He laughed. He said, "George, the first one that comes in there and says anything to you, throw him out of the office and call me. I'll take care of everything."

I said, "All right." And I did—I mean I had no problem. Red Blount became postmaster general. I'm getting ahead of myself. There's a lot of stuff.

Oh, but, yes, go with it. It's good.

I got to know Red Blount. Of course, he and Russell were great friends. And Red never give me any trouble at all, always real nice to me. The region—oh, I jumped over something but I'll go back. But there was five regions, I mean fifteen regions, and they cut them to five, I think, and they eliminated the one in Atlanta and moved it to Memphis after Russell died. So they brought a guy down here, a retired colonel, Carl Ulsacker, and he was appointing his leaders over the region. Didn't call me. Never called me. Never met him. Everybody else was appointed but me. Nothing had been done with Atlanta. All at once a letter come over—I still didn't see him, telling me where my district was going to be and in addition I'd continue as postmaster.

Of course being a presidential appointee, he couldn't do nothing about it. But they gave me the northern half of Georgia in addition to the Atlanta postmaster job. I just put it in a file, forgot it. I wouldn't look after him—I was doing what Senator Russell told me to do. Well, anyway, they moved the region to Memphis, and they called a meeting up there for all the district managers and as a postmaster district manager of the northern half of Georgia, I went up there.

And he heard you loved cheese and crackers—

Yeah, he had cheese and crackers in the car and a bottle of Jack Daniels.

He didn't know you.

I never did drink much. I guess in my lifetime I might have drank two bottles. When I first went in as postmaster every day [there was] a cocktail party somewhere in the city, like it is now. One time Mr. Duvall and I were sitting together at a cocktail party, and I didn't have a drink in my hand. He said, "George?"

I said, "Yeah?"

"Why," he said, "don't you go over there and get you a glass of orange juice? They won't know whether you're drinking or not."

So I did. He started the Atlanta Federal Reserve Bank. (J. D. Fuqua bought it. J.D. was an acquaintance of mine, too.) I took his advice. But, anyway, when Bob Gould got there, we went to my room, he'd come in and set the bottle on the desk, cheese and crackers and some juice; that's all I ever drank. I didn't have one. I have had a few drinks but not much.

But he was trying to make headway with me because he had heard, the word was out, that I was Senator Russell's boy, and nobody was going to mess with me. So I stayed on and worked at that until 1976. I started to retire. Jim Symbal, who was the regional PMG [postmaster general] at that time wanted me to—by the way, Carl Ulsacher, the guy that wouldn't even talk to me before I got to know him, he got to know me, and we became the best of friends, and he was the best manager I ever worked for. Great manager. I talked to him the other day.

So that was just some kind of oversight when he did that, [treated you that way].

He was an active Republican, and, like Senator Russell told me when I was appointed postmaster, he said, "You have become the biggest Democrat in Georgia overnight."

I said, "What's that mean?"

He said, "Don't worry about it." So I never worried about it. But I had the reputation of being the biggest Democrat in Georgia even though I had been voting Democrat all my life because we didn't know nothing else and still do most of the time.

In 1976, Jim Symbal said he wanted me to move to Memphis. And by going up there for two years I could increase my retirement $250 dollars a month. So I took it. It was the most miserable job I ever, it was the only job I ever had I didn't enjoy and didn't like. I didn't like it.

And what did you do—did you move up there?

Yeah. Moved up there, moved back in two years. But these regional jobs, there's nothing to them. Nothing to them. You sit there and talk on the phone. Just like Herman Talmadge said one time about politics—being governor of Georgia you make a decision about something you want to do and do it. But in the United States Senate you make a decision about something and talk about it. [Laughter]

And so you were up there just talking about it.

Talking about it—that's all you did.

And you didn't have the action you used to be directing.

No, no. The people in the field were the action, but it's all different now, so I don't like the way it's set up now. But I don't think I better go any farther with that.

There's a lot of things—Jim Osburn got to be a good friend of mine when I first went to the postal service when I was in charge of the data center, where we paid all the postal people in four southern states. I think he was responsible for me getting the job that I got, head of a unit there. Anyway, he and I started writing programs to consolidate, making consolidations. And he and I came up with the idea of consolidating fifteen regions in the country to five, in the postal service.

Oh, so that was your idea.

I wouldn't say it was my idea, but I was in on it. I think it might have been Mr. Lawrence who started it. He might have been the head of it, but Jim and I worked the programming out and all that stuff and decided on equipment. A lot more to that equipment we went to; it required a lot of training. But anyway, the end results were we took fifteen regions and made five regions.

Much more efficient.

Saved them several million dollars a year.

Several million dollars a year?

Yes.

Wow!

The Congress of the United States knew about Jim Osburn and me. That's one thing. There again, I didn't seek it.

Right.

Above, George speaking at a meeting in Hawaii and George and Griffin Bell. Facing page: A small sample of memorabilia from George Camp's career with the United States Postal Service.

To Henry Camp -
with best wishes,
Lyndon B. Johnson

The Inaugural Committee
requests the honor of your presence
to attend and participate in the Inauguration of

Lyndon Baines Johnson
as President of the United States of America
and
Hubert Horatio Humphrey
as Vice President of the United States of America
on Wednesday the twentieth of January
one thousand nine hundred and sixty five
in the City of Washington

Dale Miller
Chairman

THE WHITE HOUSE
WASHINGTON

Tokyo, Japan
May 1, 1986

Dear Governor Camp:

I have signed the Acts of the Nineteenth Congress of the
Universal Postal Union, negotiated at Hamburg in 1984, but
I want us now to make sure that the Acts, and particularly
Article 23, are not used to stifle healthy private competi-
tion in the international mail arena. The policy of this
Administration is to encourage free enterprise in ways that
will improve services and reduce costs to our citizens, and
I know I can count on your support to carry out this policy.

Therefore, I am asking that you do all within your power,
working closely with the Executive Branch, especially the
Secretary of State and the Attorney General, to permit and
promote marketplace competition in international mail, and
to influence other nations to do likewise.

Sincerely,

Ronald Reagan

The Honorable George W. Camp
Board of Governors
United States Postal Service
11950 Chaffin Road
Roswell, Georgia 30075-1450

CHAPTER 19

The Postal Board of Governors: Nominations, Investigations & Senate Confirmation

I have a lot of things here that we didn't finish: my career. We stopped before we got to the appointment to the Board of Governors.

Right. Let's start there.

Mr. Lawrence was the guy who always pushed me; I don't know why. When I retired from active duty he wanted me to get on the board, the Board of Governors of the United States Postal Service. Well, he started a drive to get me appointed by the president. He called Phil Alston, who was head of a law firm, Alston & Bird, here in Atlanta. And he was

The United States Postal Service Board of Governors, 1985.

"This board, appointed by the president with the advice and consent of the Senate, represents the public interest. It directs the exercise of the powers of the Postal Service, directs and controls its expenditures, reviews its practices, conducts long-range planning and sets policies on all postal matters. It is comparable to a board of directors of a public corporation." (From the official Board of Governors brochure, 1985.)

Seated, left to right: Peter Voss, John McKean, Al Casey (Postmaster General)
Standing, left to right: John Ryan, George Camp, Jackie Strange (Deputy Postmaster General), Tyler McConnell, Ruth Peters, Robert Setrakian, and John Griesemer

ambassador to Australia. And then all the postmasters in Georgia and Alabama, they worked on him, and he got all of them to endorse me, the different senators.

Why do you think he did that?

I don't know. I don't know.

He started that, and all the postmasters in Georgia and Alabama who worked for me and a lot of them across the country that I had become acquainted with and knew was pushing it because President Carter was from Georgia. And they knew I knew him when he was the governor of Georgia.

And I was really investigated because the postmaster general and some of his staff in Washington didn't want me on there because of my knowledge and background of the post office. In fact, seventeen postal inspectors checked me from beginning to end. Everything I'd ever done. Trying to find out something. And they checked the promotional procedures that I used, and they compared them with the other offices across the country.

And as it turned out, I promoted more blacks than anybody else in the large offices. But I only promoted people who could do the job. If they didn't, I'd demote them. And I had that reputation across the country, demoting people. Not only blacks but whites—if they didn't do the job, I demoted them. But, anyway, it took a year—well, over a year, about fifteen months.

All this time I was being investigated, and, finally, one day I picked up the *Wall Street Journal* and I'd been nominated by the president— nomination sent to the Senate made me nominated. And in two or three weeks I got the letter from Senator Glenn—he was chairman of the committee that I had gone before—and I had to fill out a bunch of papers and submit them up there. I had to do that two or three times and had to go to the White House and meet with the personnel director up there and meet with several of the staff of the president. And finally after going through all these procedures and complying with all the wishes, whatever they wanted me to do, I was called by the Senate for confirmation. And I went before the Senate. They worked me over pretty good. There were people that I knew. Of course you've seen these committee meetings; you know how they work over the candidates.

George at airport, 1971.

Do you remember how that felt?

Oh, yeah. [Laughter] I felt pretty small. You look up to them; see, the senators are sitting up higher than you are. You look up to them. And after I guess an hour and a half—there were three of us being confirmed at that time—the meeting was over, and I left.

Do you remember any questions that were difficult for you or—

Oh, no. No problem. I answered every question. I had no problem because I knew what I was doing. I'd been postmaster, acting postmaster. But I went to the airport, got on the plane, come home. Hadn't been home long, a week or so, I got a call from some gentleman I didn't know, wanted to see me in Washington. So I went up there. Went to his office. He was an assistant to one of the senators, I found out later. And one of the individuals, I'd rather not name his name. He was pretty rough on me because he said I was too hard on people and I made them work. He tried his best to get me turned down.

But I was surprised. I wasn't expecting nothing like that. I didn't know I was that unreasonable because I had no problem here running the office. But I found out it was a grudge. He had a grudge against me, and I didn't know it. He was on the staff of the postmaster general. And so after he finished, again, I went to Senator Russell and told him about this meeting. He laughed and said, "Don't worry about it." So I come home. No it wasn't Senator Russell I went to, no, no, it was some other;

it was Senator Talmadge. Senator Russell had already died then. But he said, "Don't worry about that." So I come home.

About a week later I got a phone call; I'd been confirmed. But after that hearing—there was three of us to be confirmed—when I came out of the building, there was a limousine sitting there. And two young fellows who worked in the White House grabbed me by the arm and pushed me in the limousine. They didn't get the other two. That really upset those other two. They didn't know what was happening. But they drove away like they didn't tell them. And I went about two blocks, and they said we just wanted to create an impression.

Oh! My—

They didn't know what it was all about, I thought, so I guess you created it. [Laughter] So they let me out, and I went to the hotel and got my baggage, and I come home. [Laughter] But those two other guys—you can imagine the rumors that were floating around during that time because I had some opposition at that time and I wasn't going to worry about it until it all come about. Because they thought I was going to try to take over the board when I went up there.

CHAPTER 20

In the Corridors of Power

And so that was in November, I think, or October. No. It was October—
went up there for the board meeting in October. And I walked in the
postal service, and I'd checked in a hotel. I'd been briefed where to go
and all that business. DuPont Plaza hotel across the street from the post
office, they put us all on the top floor in suites, first class, nice. We always
met in the evening, at seven o'clock in the evening when we went to a
meeting. I went up there about a quarter of seven and walked in—the
postmaster general was talking to a man there, who I didn't know. And
he brought me out and said, "Hey, George, come on over."

I went over, and he said, "I want you to meet Mike Wright; he's our
chairman of the board." I sat there and talked to him a little bit. Mike

Wright was chairman of Exxon Corporation. Well, he was chairman of both the boards. That meeting—I kind of sat still for a meeting or two and didn't have much to say. Then maybe in October, November, or December, very quiet. January meeting we elect a chairman. First week in January for the coming year. They were all expecting me to go for that chairmanship because President Carter's from Georgia and was a friend of mine. I walked in there—and this opened my eyes—I didn't let them know it.

One of them says, "I nominate Mike Wright," and the other one says, "I second," and another one said, "I move that the nominations be closed." Just like that. I didn't say a word. When they asked for a vote, I voted for Mike Wright. I knew what was going on all that time. But later I found out, there was a fellow, worked in Stuart Eisenstadt's office—I don't know whether you heard of Stuart Eisenstadt. He was very active in the Carter campaign, and he was an ambassador someplace during the Clinton administration. And he's on TV right now. He was keeping the postmaster general informed, this fellow that worked for him, on my status. And I knew about this through my sources at the White House.

So Mike's term ran out in 1980, I guess, and we had to elect a new chairman because his term ran out. He wasn't on the board anymore. And we were down in I believe it was Dallas, no; it was Austin, down in Austin, Texas. It was time to nominate another chairman. I'd been getting all kind of publicity that I was going to be the next chairman, going to be the postmaster general and all this stuff. I never said a word about it. It was a rumor, you know. Things go on during [times like that]; they didn't know what I was going to do. When they opened the floor for nominations, I spoke up and nominated Bob Hardesty for chairman. That knocked them off their feet.

And who was he?

He was on the staff with President Lyndon Johnson during his administration. And he was also a member of the board. And he had several years to go, so I nominated him.

I bet the people were so surprised. You hadn't said anything to anybody, had you—

He was, too. He told me since several times, you knocked me off of my feet. He thought I was going to seek it. But I knew that I couldn't be elected because there were so many board members who'd been appointed by people who were opposed to me. And the reason they were opposed to me I know, and I'll get into that later. But, anyway, we went on for several years with Bob, and then when Bob retired as chairman, we elected a new chairman, a member that President Ronald Reagan had nominated.

But you were still on the board.

Oh, yeah, I was still on the board. And John McKean had been chairman under the Reagan administration. He was chief accountant for Reagan's attorney general, Ed Meese.

This new crowd that came in—see, board members are appointed for nine-year terms or what was left of them [terms] that had expired, and you serve nine years plus one additional year if nobody had been appointed to replace you. But, anyway, after the Reagan people came in, one a year was supposed to be appointed and the board was made up of five members of the party in power and four members of the party out of power. So there were nine on the board. Anyway, I was treated much better under the Reagan administration than I was under the Carter administration because the board members under the Carter administration had been appointed by Nixon.

One night we'd had a meeting, and somebody knocked on my door—I'd gone back to the hotel—it was the chairman and another member wanted to talk to me. And because I was re-elected on the board by that time, I knew what was going on, and I did a lot of questioning about appointments and mail processing and why things cost so much and budget and all that stuff because I knew what I was doing. And they were outsiders. I was the only postal man on the board. And John McKean said, "George, I'd like you to be vice chairman."

I said, "These people won't vote for me for vice chairman."

"You let me handle that," he said. "Will you accept it?"

I said, "Yeah, I'll accept it."

So the next morning when it was time to come up for election, they elected me vice chairman. That surprised me, too. [Laughter] But then

I served the rest of my term which was supposed to expire in '85, I think. I had an extra year because the year before Reagan had appointed somebody else. And then after that was over, I was vice-chairman of the postal service. So that ends it.

Well, that's really a lesson in behind-the-scenes politics.

Oh, yes. But during the time I was on that board we appeared every year before the house committee and the senate committee on the operations of the postal service. And they were—of course, they always question the chairman. The rest of us was sitting there. And one day I was sitting there, and I was kind of smiling a little bit because they'd given him a rough time. And one of the senators, I forget the senator's name, said to me, "What are you smiling about?"

"Well," I said, "I just thought that was a silly question." [Laughter]

Did everybody laugh?

Everybody laughed, including him. It was the, I'll tell you who it was; it was the senator from Alaska. Anyway, we went to Alaska on several meetings. He had us up there, and we went to his house in Washington, had dinner and visited with them.

He's still a senator now, isn't he?

Yeah.

Yes, and he is very active at promoting his state. He's very good at that.

Yes, he's very active. But, anyway, he had an accident, a plane accident, and his wife got killed in that accident. He survived, and he married again. He had the cutest little girl you ever laid your eyes on. She was about ten years old that time we went to dinner at his home. Getting back to those trips, every time we went to Anchorage, he'd have several hundred people in the evening for dinner and a party for us. And one night I was sitting there eating, I finished up, and somebody tapped me on the shoulder, and I looked around and it was a lady, and she asked me who I was and I told her. She said, "Are you from Georgia?"

I said, "Yes."

She said, "Do you know Chip Vandiver?"

"No," I said, "but I know his father, ex-governor Vandiver of Georgia."

She said, "Chip is my husband."

I said, "Is he here?"

"No," She said, "he's out of town. Come on, let's dance." [Laughter] So I danced with her.

Then what amazed me on those trips, I learned so much about Alaska. You know just about all the transportation is by plane. Shipping Coca-Cola's by post office on those little planes, to different locations all over the state of Alaska.

Really.

Yeah, everything. By post office. And the American people subsidizing it.

And you didn't approve of that—

No, I didn't. I questioned about it. I questioned about it. But that senator was awfully nice to me. He was real nice. Because he knew I'd ask him questions about that stuff. I didn't back off. Building post offices, the postmaster general wanted to be on the inside because he was the one who approved things that we needed from the Congress and the Senate. And he'd build a post office for them if it was needed. And I've always questioned it. Why was it needed? And they'd have to justify it to me before I recommended to the board to approve it. I didn't have the authority to approve or disapprove nothing. The board would do that.

But how valuable to have your perspective, a person who was an insider.

Letter-sorting equipment and staff, January 1968.

CHAPTER 21

I Handled It

Let's talk about the mechanization that, the things that started when you were with the post office. And the Life of Georgia project where you did the vertical—

Yes. Well, you mean the mail-handling equipment?

Right. It's so mechanized now, but it was coming from very hands-on to—

Before I left we started that and got one-line readers as part of the first mechanization; I think we got four, five, or six of them. And they've been improved drastically since then. I was a part of that. I was on the Board of Governors. I was on the committee where Ruth Peters and me worked continuously on that, to upgrade the machinery.

And was there much resistance at the beginning?

Oh. yeah. Oh, yeah. Yeah.

How did you handle that?

Well, we just had to go ahead. It had to be done because the volume was growing and continues to grow, doesn't grow in proportion to what it used to because there's so many other means now of getting your message out. But it's still a lot of mail, a lot of mail. But a lot of people pay their bills now electronically. I don't. I still use the mail. But you still have a lot of first-class mail. And this other mail you use for filling in your labor force. Post office, still, I don't know whether the people in this country realize how important it is to them and how useful it is.

Right, but if we had to go without it a few days we would start to—

Yes, yes.

Well, the thing that got me most, I guess, that I enjoyed more than anything else was when mechanization was going on in that period. Ruth Peters—who was in personnel in the post office department before she was appointed on the board—Ruth was a fine lady. Real active Republican from Louisiana. But she was appointed chairman of the committee to look into mechanization. And she asked that I be her assistant chairman and then appointed me vice-chairman.

And they had some one-line readers which only read one line on the letter. Well, that was not sufficient, but some hanky panky went on. I never was able to find out what it was. But, anyway, I got started. We killed that and bought new readers; now we have three-line readers. But there was one of the governors got involved with some contractors, and they were trying to do some shady work.

And get that one-line reader in?

No, he was backing us up, but he was getting paid off. Or he wanted to get paid off, but he didn't get paid off. That was his intent. Anyway, they caught him. And he served four years in prison. And you talk about investigating. Now they investigated me and Ruth Peters about that contract from beginning to end. Like we had something to do with it. But I sat here on my porch and inspectors come out and talked to me.

But you could hold your own because you hadn't done anything wrong.

Didn't do anything wrong. Just did what I was supposed to do. But that was really interesting. They've improved it some since I left. But it was started—Ruth Peters who was chairman, and I was vice-chairman of that mechanization committee, and we started that. That is the one-line reader part. We had sorters, operators that sat there and keyed it in beforehand. But on these readers you just let it go through, and you've got cancellation. Got a lot of them now. They're operating good, too.

Did any other senators invite the board to their state?

Not like Ted Stephens. He had us to Alaska several times. Three or four times we had board meetings up there.

Well, he was on the committee, the chair—

We went to Hawaii two or three times. And I went over there several times to make speeches to conventions, NAPUS, the National Association of Postmasters of the United States and the other postmasters organization. I went over there one time and talked to them. And they had a national meeting over there.

And so when you would do something like that, what would you speak on, the current state of the—

Post office, what we were doing and the plans, our condition, financial condition, and what we hoped to accomplish in the future and why, if we were going to raise the postage and why, and all that stuff. See the board, we was the one that raised the price of stamps. And I fought that with everything I had until they showed me we had to have it.

During my time on that board President Reagan asked for and got a supplement from the post office, and I don't remember what it was all about. But anyway, the post office gives him a good bit of money. I don't know whether they still do that or not. [The money comes] out of their account, the budget. I don't know whether that's still going on or not. But I hated to see that, do that and then raise the price of a stamp. Because when I was postmaster a stamp was three cents. Now it will be forty-one cents next year. Good Lord.

Do you have any opinions—as a person out of the business now, but who knew the business so well when you were in it—do you have some opinions about things the way they are today?

Well, I thought we did a better job, but, in other words, when I—I'd rather not say anything to criticize what they are doing now because I don't know. But I do know when I ran the Atlanta district and the Atlanta postmaster job, I had seven staff members and I had most of Georgia, 95% of the state of Alabama, and I handled all of it. And led the Southern region in the country in productivity in mail handling. And I know that, and it's a matter of record at the post office.

When they replaced me, they replaced me and my staff of ten people, with, oh, I don't know thirty, thirty-five managers. And the Atlanta postmaster now doesn't have a thing to do with anything except stations and branches delivering the mail. He doesn't have transportation, he doesn't have mail handling—that's all handled by somebody else. I don't know enough about it now to talk about it other than the fact that the postmaster doesn't have the responsibility and authority that I had when I was there. And I don't think this is as good. I think one person should run it all.

That does seem to make sense, that you'd have a vision of all the interlocking parts.

They kept expanding my range of responsibility, tried to get me loaded down, but I handled it.

CHAPTER 22

Tom Mix, Johnny B.,
and Old Maude

Let's just switch gears a little bit and just talk about, in general, some firsts in your life or memories that were either first or most memorable in terms of things out in the culture, like do you remember the first movie you ever saw or an early movie?

I remember going to Dallas on Saturday evenings, seeing Tom Mix movies. Those were the ones I loved. Cost a dime. I didn't have a dime every Saturday. Every once in a while I'd get to go. I'd walk four miles.

Walk four miles to the movies—

See a movie and go home. That was before we had any transportation other than mules and a wagon.

And was it at night?

It was on Saturday afternoon. Sometimes it was night. We had to work, which we did most of the time. We had to work. I loved those Tom Mix movies. They had one theater there, and most of the young people would go see them.

And when you went was somebody else along, some of the other kids in the family, of course they were younger—

No, no. I was the only one. I'd go by myself.

And when you got there, you'd see people you knew.

Oh, yeah. I knew everybody in the county. There weren't that many people. [Laughter]

Right. And how about, I know you had animals, farm animals, but were there any of the animals that you might have considered special or a pet?

Well, I had a horse. Rode him bareback. I'd go in the pasture and holler, and he'd come. I had a horse up until about ten years old.

Did you have a name for it?

Maude.

Maude.

Old Maude.

And how about friends, buddies—

Oh, yeah. I had a lot of friends. My cousin Johnny B. We stayed together from the time, I guess, we was five or six years old, spent 90% of our time together until we was seventeen. We had a bad experience during those times. His daddy owned the Chevrolet place—that was my daddy's brother—in Dallas. For some reason he come to Atlanta and started to own a restaurant on Marietta Street, and his family moved someplace out there. And one day a waitress got in a fight in his restaurant, and the police come, and he got in a fight with the police. And he shot a policeman, and the policeman shot him. And Johnny B. was at my house. Kept him. And we had a hard time with Johnny B. then. That was 1930, I guess.

From then on just about every summer John B. and I were together, and we fished together, we hunted together, went to the movies together. We did everything together. We dated together.

Okay. What about a first possession that you felt like was yours that was important to you.

First possession—

Might have been a gift or—

Well, I had a dog, dogs. Beagle dogs. That's growing up; they were rabbit dogs. Back in those days, shells cost you a nickel apiece. Daddy gave me a single-barrel shotgun—Ronnie has it now, at his house—but you couldn't afford to miss when you shot. You had to kill them. And you'd get fifteen cents for them or three gun shells.

That attitude is part of your secret of success, too. You've got one shot; you've got to make it—

Because if you missed, you lost a nickel. [Laughter] I did a lot of hunting; I guess my rabbit dogs is the first thing I thought of as mine.

What about things out in the world like popular songs or that sort of thing as you were growing up. Do you remember any of those?

No, we didn't have a radio. We didn't have a radio when I left home. When I left home we still didn't have electricity or indoor plumbing.

Oh, and at those Saturday dances you had live music. And they probably did a lot of traditional songs.

Oh, yeah. "Down Yonder" and all that stuff.

What do you think of the importance of music out in the world today for young people and—

I don't like what I hear. I like the '40s and '50s and '60s. That's me. I'm old fashioned. I like gospel. I love gospel.

So do you go to church now?

Mount Vernon Baptist Church. In Sandy Springs, been out there since 1968. Prior to that went to Beecher Hills in southwest Atlanta.

Ron Camp on the day his father was sworn in as Atlanta's postmaster.

CHAPTER 23

Ronnie

You want me to go on some more?

Of course, sure.

You know when I got out of the service and I found that apartment, we lived there four years. Martha was working, and I was working. I bought several cars and sold them, and then I bought a new '49 Ford. She paid the Ford off, and we bought a lot and I paid the lot off. Every payday, we'd pay the note. We decided [to have a baby], and then Ronnie was born in 1950 on April 17th.

We stayed in that apartment until our home on Pollard Drive was almost finished. Two weeks after he was born, we moved in. And we had the first house, built the first house on Pollard Drive. And that was the highlight of my life as far as having a brick home and everything.

That must have been exciting.

Oh, yeah. We had a washer and dryer for the first time in our life. It was exciting. I was working at McPherson at that time, and I had to teach Martha how to drive shortly thereafter. She didn't know how to drive. I taught her how to drive in that '49 Ford. It would rattle and roll; there wasn't much to it, but it was a new car. That was back when the American automobile dealers could sell anything they built, before the Japaneses came in here with their cars. But I lived there until 1968. And I had met Howard Chatham. I don't know whether you've ever heard of Howard Chatham.

I may have heard that name.

He owned Northside Realty. He built more than 50,000 homes: he built North Atlanta, actually. And he wanted me to move over here.

To what used to be the country.

What used to be the country. He built my house in Sandy Springs. In 1967 I went and built there, but Martha wouldn't move because Ronnie was going to Woodward Academy, and he had another year. Are you familiar with Woodward Academy?

Yes.

And she wouldn't take it, so I told Howard I had to sell it, and he sold it. The next year he built me another one, on another lot. Ronnie graduated from Woodward that year, and we moved out to Sandy Springs in August—I think it was August of 1968, right after he graduated.

And, of course, he went away to college, but before he went away he was working during the summers. I'd get him a job at IBM or for a surveying company or J.C. Penney. He had several different jobs. But I never will forget the first year he went to college. Ronnie was full of mischief. He loved having a good time. Didn't get in any trouble. If he got in trouble, I didn't know about it. But one night he come home, first year in college; he hadn't done well. "I'm going to quit school."

Oh, I wasn't going to argue with him. I said, "Okay, son, you get up at 5:30 in the morning and go to work for me. You'll have a job tomorrow." He went off some place (I'd bought him a car). I heard him come back about nine o'clock and get his clothes and left. He'd gone back to school. [Laughter] But you know he never made another B.

Really!

The first year he just barely passed. But he made straight A's the last three years in college.

Wow!

I was so proud of that young man.

You obviously inspired something there with the job offer.

I was so proud of him.

A lot of kids don't do well the first year. But I don't think I've ever heard of someone turning around as quickly as that.

When he graduated from college, I took him down to Muse's. I said, "Son, pick you out some clothes." He got four suits of clothes, maybe two, three, or four. A bunch of shirts, ties. And I'd already had him some appointments set up. George Thorpe of National Data was a friend of mine. He talked to him about a job, and he talked to Ed Smith, who was chairman of First National Bank. Ed wanted him to come in as a trainee for the bank. Officer trainee, I guess. He turned that down. I thought it was a good job. I didn't try to influence him. He turned it down and went to work for National Data. He didn't stay out there long; he left after a few months. He quit and he and Jim Johnson and Ray Miller started Southeastern Data. Well, Jim died and Ray retired, and now Ronnie is president.

Sounds like that was a good decision—

They did not have any business at all when they started. They went in debt, had a rough time, but I'm so proud of that young man. He's got a lot of my traits; I can see them every time I'm around him. I hope I influenced him some. I'm real proud of him. When I bought him those clothes at Muse's, I said, "Okay, son, you're on your own now." That booger has done all right.

Oh, that's a good story.

Alan Camp on the day his father was sworn in as Atlanta's postmaster.

CHAPTER 24

Alan

Oh, Ronnie went to West Georgia College. I forgot to mention that. Alan was born in 1954, a good, good child. I keep remembering his long, curly hair. The first, I think seventh grade, maybe eighth grade, he went to Southwest High School and when we moved to Sandy Springs, he didn't know anybody. It was kind of rough on him. And he didn't like that, you know teenagers, and I bought him a scooter. He'd put gas in that thing; he'd tear it apart and put it back together. But he'd run all over Sandy Springs. But during that period of time, Ronnie was away in college.

So Alan got to be an only child for a while.

He was an only child for a while. And I was traveling a lot, and he really looked after his mother a lot. If he had a date he'd come home; he'd bring the dates home. He grew up and finished high school at North Springs. And when he finished high school at North Springs, he wanted to go to Furman University. I said, "Son, you can't go to Furman University."

He said, "Why?"

"You can't get in," I said.

"If I can get in," he said, "Can I go?"

I said yes. And he got in. [Laughter]

That was a good challenge.

He got in, and he went up there for three years. He didn't do too well. He passed. He had to fail a few subjects, but he did all right. But then he transferred to Georgia, and it took him two years to finish. That chemistry business and all that. And the boy across the street from us—who was he with? One of the pharmaceutical firms, Eli Lilly—done very well. I think once Alan—he didn't want no part of government. Alan didn't, neither did Ronnie. Alan applied with Ciba-Geigy, and they hired him. And he stayed with them for twenty-five years.

Well, that's quite a company.

And he's worked on—for the last twenty years—cancer drugs for different types of cancer, cancer drugs. He's been with several different companies. Done real well. Got a great gal.

They have a daughter who's a senior at Georgia now, and she wants to go into medicine. Apparently, she's trying to get in Emory. She's already been through the first two steps, and I don't know if she's going to make it or not. And their son is graduating this year from Roswell High School. I don't know where he's going to college. He's 6' 4". All he thinks about is baseball. He's a baseball pitcher. Of course, Ronnie's got two sons and a girl.

Well, that's great! So five grandchildren—

Oh, yeah. Ronnie's second son is majoring in chemistry at Georgia Southern. And his daughter, Natalie, is at Jacksonville State in Alabama. I didn't get involved in any of that. Stayed away from all of that. I always told my boys to go wherever they want to. And Ronnie told me he was going to Tennessee. I said, "Okay, son, if you can get in." But, in the meantime, he met Pat. And he changed his mind and went to West Georgia because he'd be home, could come home and see Pat.

Oh, fate works in strange ways. To change our lives.

Oh, yeah. Used to pick her up and come to the house. We had a real nice basement set up. He'd go down there in the evening and study.

Okay, Brad. You were saying something about your grandson Brad while we had a break—

Brad is a technician; he works for Ronnie. He's a real, real good computer man.

Let me name all my grandchildren: Brad, Meredith, David, Natalie, and Matthew.

That's a nice crop of grandchildren.

Pat's gone back to college now that the kids are gone. Alan's wife, Debbie, is a flight attendant, has been with Delta over twenty-five years. I'm so blessed. I am so blessed. My family's done so well. Good Lord blessed me beyond all means, and I know it. Especially with my wife. She raised my kids. She is the love of my life.

CHAPTER 25

Real Networking

When I went in as postmaster, my regional director had a meeting of the large post offices in the Atlanta region, which included north and south Atlanta, Georgia, and Florida. And the postmasters of the largest offices, I guess fifteen or twenty, would meet every three or four months to discuss operations and budgets and man hours and what have you. And so when they would come to Atlanta, my job was to find them a place to stay.

You were the host.

I was host in our district, and at that time I believe we was getting eleven dollars per diem. And I put them in the Americana Hotel, which was the only new hotel in downtown Atlanta at that time. We had to pay seven dollars per night. And they had four dollars to eat lunch on. And, of course, we took them to the baseball game or something like that—I knew the owner of the team and I could get free tickets, take them to a baseball game.

During the day we'd have meetings. And I got to know the people at the Americana. Dr. Olson Smith owned the Americana. Andy Naples, who was a member of my church, had the food and beverage concession at the Americana Hotel. I'd go down there quite often and have lunch with him. One day I walked in to have lunch with Andy, and I heard somebody. He said, "Hey, George." I turned around and there's ex-governor Ellis Arnall. He said, "Come here." I walked over, and he said, "I want you to meet Walt Disney."

Oh! Walt Disney!

And I said, "Good to see you, Mr. Disney. What on earth brings you to our wonderful state?"

He said, "Well, we've been looking for property."

And I said, "What are they going to do with property, governor?"

And Mr. Disney said, "We're going to build Disney World somewhere."

I said, "I hope you found it here."

He said, "Well, we looked at three or four locations here," said, "we're going to Florida tomorrow."

"What are you going to Florida for?" I said. "You don't need to go to Florida. Stay here." None of this had been in the paper. So we chatted fifteen, twenty minutes. And I went on to my lunch, and they went to Florida. Two weeks later the Florida deal was announced.

Oh, my goodness. I wonder where in Georgia they might have put it.

Someplace in Douglas County was one of them. I don't know where else.

I never heard about that before this. That is so interesting.

Yeah, and I used to go, after he built it; of course, he died not too long after that. But he looked healthy to me that day. (I was taller than he was.) But he looked great. Had a nice chat, and I really enjoyed talking with him. But after that I was down there with the post office, stuff like that. Quite a few times. On several occasions I'd go down there and one time I went down there with George Cagle, Cagle Poultry, have you heard of it?

Oh, yes.

George is a friend of mine, at church, and Doug Cagle still runs Cagle's over here. George told me and Andy, says, "I'm going to put my company on the market tomorrow. Three dollars a share." I have an IPO.

Andy says, "I want 500 shares."

"Okay," George says. "You got it."

And I said, "Give me a hundred." I got a hundred, but I didn't keep them. I sold them.

But Andy died, oh, after he opened PittyPat's Porch—he and Anthony, you've heard of Anthony's Restaurants. And Anthony was his partner at that time. And they had a hundred thousand dollars life insurance on just one of them if the other one died. So when Andy died, Anthony got the—this is so, Andy Naples told me about this, that's how I know. So Mary Naples, Andy's wife, died about three months ago. He was a good friend.

We had a lot of meetings with that crowd of postmasters in the region. I had a lot of good friends in that group. But now getting away from just the region, there was, I believe, it was eighty-six large offices nationwide, and we went to Washington or someplace in the country and had three or four meetings a year. And I got to meet all of these postmasters of large offices across the country. Became friends with all of them.

Right—it was a real network for you.

Oh, yes, a real network. And we would compare how we were doing. To begin with I didn't, but the last few years I did. I really enjoyed that. And when Jimmy Carter run for president—this is real interesting. I called them all. Talked to Red Nunnally one day, from Omaha, Nebraska, and he said, "George, Jimmy Carter is coming down here to have a meeting at my restaurant." He had a restaurant and was also the postmaster.

I said, "You tell him I called you and asked you to vote for him."

I ran into Carter after that at a campaign event, and he said, "You sure know a lot of people." [Laughter]

He's going all around the country, and he's running into people that you know.

So I made a lot of friendships. And I traveled all over the country, not only with the big regional offices, but also with the National Organization of Postmasters of the United States. They'd have meetings or conventions and I'd go to those. So I had a lot of good experiences, met a lot of great people. I really enjoyed it.

And I bet that really was fun and rewarding in the later years because you knew the job. You knew the people. You knew their circumstances, and you'd been to where they live and that sort of thing. That must have been great.

Another great friend I had was Marvin Shoob, my lawyer and friend. Marvin's still sitting on the bench, Judge Shoob. Marvin and I had a lot of good times together, a lot of experience. Tried to start several projects, but we never was able to finish them. When I bought my house, he closed it out. Paid him for the closing costs and at the closing place, three days later he mailed the check back to me. Never would take nothing.

Oh, how nice!

He was still an attorney at that time before he became a judge. And he swore me in when I was appointed to the board of governors, the postal service board, and had to be sworn in by a judge. And, of course, Marvin was financial manager to Sam Nunn when he ran for the Senate first time. Of course, I helped him all I could. But I couldn't be too active with that.

CHAPTER 26

American Presidents

And this is something—I'm bouncing around.

Oh that's fine.

I was in Memphis when I was in the regional office.

Oh, that brief time when you moved from Georgia—

Yeah. Anyway, Paul Burke called me and says, "George, President Carter's going to lose Louisiana."

I said, "What do you mean?"

George with Sam Harris accepting a Postal Employees Day proclamation from Governor Jimmy Carter, April 23, 1973.

"He's going to lose it." The day before the governor's wife had went down to Mississippi with Gerald Ford on the boat, you know.

I said, "What can we do about that, Paul?"

He said, "I'll tell you what." (Paul was postmaster of New Orleans.) He said, "If he'll come down here and call the sheriffs of every county, all the sheriffs in Louisiana together and have a meeting with them," he said, "they can turn it around."

So I said "I'll see what I can do." So when he hung up, I called Phil Austin. I told him what Paul had told me. He said, "You think that'll work?"

"I don't know, Phil," I said, "I'm just passing on to you what I heard." I don't know what he did or if he did anything. I don't know. But, anyway, a few days later, I read in the paper where Carter was meeting with the sheriffs in Louisiana. Now I don't know whether I started that or not. Anyway, the next morning after the election Louisiana put Carter in as president. It was the last state.

Wow. So interesting how a little something here, a little something there—

Yeah. That happened.

Well, I bet that was fun reading that about Louisiana, during the returns.

Oh, Mr. Duvall. We mentioned that the other day about the Atlanta Federal, Mr. Duvall, about that drinking?

Oh, yes.

I checked on his name: Mr. Duvall. Another thing, Millsby Lane was a good friend of mine. He gave me that party when I was sworn in as postmaster. And he always wanted me to get involved in something to make some money because he knew in government employment you didn't make a lot of money; you're comfortable, but you don't get rich. And several times he'd have something he'd repossessed and he'd say, "All you've got to do is sign your name, take it over."

I'd say, "Mills, I can't do that." I said, "These papers will eat me up. They'll throw me out of town." I never did.

And they would have when you were having all those investigations.

That's right. They would. But one day he called me and that was back when I had to sign all absentee ballots—anybody that'd cast a ballot that way, me or a judge or somebody had to sign it. I don't know whether you remember those days or not. He called me. He said, "Come out here. I want you to sign my ballot."

"Okay," I said. "Where are you?" His office was across the street. He said he was at home. I went out there, and he said, "George, I'm leaving tomorrow."

I said, "Where in the world you going?"

He said, "I'm going home."

"You going to Savannah?"

"Yep," he said.

I said, "What are you quitting for?"

He said, "I had a slight heart attack, and it's time for me to go." So I signed his ballot, and I talked to him several times, but I never did see him anymore, talked to him on the phone. I hated that.

He's figured in a number of stories we've heard. It sounds like he was always watching out for people and trying to help communities in Georgia.

President John F. Kennedy—I thought he was a great man.

Me, too.

I thought he was a great president. I never had the pleasure of actually meeting him. I talked to him on the phone.

You did?

He sent me that picture [indicating a framed photo on the wall].

I was at Steve Dunna's restaurant on Lucky Street, having lunch with the postmaster of Jacksonville and the postmaster of Orlando one day and Steve come over, and he said, "George!"

I said, "Yeah."

He said, "The president's just been shot." And that scared me. I just pushed my plate away. Then we just got up and left. We went back to the regional office; we was having a meeting with the officers. And we just sit there all afternoon, nobody—there wasn't any talking. That was a sad, sad, sad day. And Johnny Carter, who worked in the region, come by about 4:30. He told me, he says, "I'm going to Washington." The president's already died, and Lyndon Johnson's been sworn in. Johnny was catching the train and going to Washington. Johnny was a good friend.

I said, "When will you be back?"

He said, "I don't know—a week or so." Well, that upset the regional director; he didn't want Johnny to go. And I didn't know at that time that Cliff Carter, who was Johnny's brother, was going to be Lyndon Johnson's chief of staff. But Johnny went up there and then they told him they was going to bring him to Washington and put him in charge of all the regions in the post office. Boy, he went [snaps fingers] like that!

So he was there for longer than a week.

Oh. yeah. He was there a long time. [Laughter]

The Varsity, July 1958.

Lane Brothers Commercial Photographers Collection, Special Collections Department, Georgia State University Library.

CHAPTER 27

A Good Place to Be

[Looking through a guest book from his office when he was postmaster.]

Colonel Barrington was a great friend of mine. He retired Lt. Colonel in the army. He was real close to Carl Sanders and Charlie Weltner and Herman Talmadge.

Now the beginning date here is 6/3/66.

Two or three years they didn't have it. Lots of postmasters here. My memory's not very good. I don't remember these people. A lot of people come in, and all of them didn't see me. I directed some of them to the staff. There's no way I could see all these people.

When I had an appointment with somebody, if they wasn't there on time, they didn't see me. I closed the door. When I went somewhere, I'm there on time or I don't go. I've always been that way. I can't help it.

So a typical day you would be in the office and you would have—

I was there at seven o'clock every morning. And normally I would go to lunch with somebody or else I'd go to—Herb Jenkins, the police chief, would pick me up a lot of times, and we'd go out to The Varsity and eat with Frank Gordy, who owned The Varsity. Herb would call him and he'd have us two hot dogs and onion rings in his office, and we'd sit there and talk to him. Frank was a great guy. I wasn't supposed to do this, but he'd call me sometimes when he was going to hire someone and he'd say, "George, did he ever work for you?"

"I don't know," I'd say. "I'll check it out."

He'd say, "Let me know if I should hire him."

And I'd say, "Frank, I can't do that."

And he'd say, "You just say hire him or don't hire him."

I said, "Okay."

I guess it was part of getting references. So you had a whole network going there of people that trusted each other.

[Laughter] I was right downtown. I was on a first-name basis with everybody. It was a good place to be. A lot of good things happened to you. [Continuing to look through the guest book, with pages of names.] Headquarters. A lot of people from Washington in here. I can remember the face but—I remember Norman, Oklahoma; Memphis; Jacksonville. Lord have mercy. Las Vegas.

D.C.

Oh, yeah. I can't get much out of this book.

Well, it was interesting to get that story about your lunches at The Varsity.

Oh, yeah. [Still going through book] New York, everywhere else.

So many names—

CHAPTER 28

A Tense Time at the Post Office

Oh, one thing I didn't tell you about. When I went in as postmaster, a day or two later, I didn't know how it happened, but Ivan Allen called and he asked me to come over to his office. I went over there, and he said, "George, you're going to have problems."

And I said, "I know. I'm going to have plenty of them."

He said, "Well, let me tell you something. Don't let this situation get to you." He says, "Be firm and fair. If people earn something, give it to them. If they don't, don't worry about it." But, he said, "As long as you're firm and fair, you're going to catch—well, they're going to raise cane with you whatever happens."

But the first three years I was in my office, the black newspapers and the *Atlanta Constitution* gave me a hard time. I couldn't do anything right.

Okay. So the first three years they gave you a hard time—

The black newspapers, the Atlanta newspapers, the black union, and the blacks in general gave me a hard time. I could do nothing to please them. Every time they'd have a function of any type, they'd ask me to go. I'd go. I'd treat them right. I didn't mistreat them. When they did a good job, I promoted them. You know if they earned it, but if they hadn't earned it, I didn't.

And that was your policy.

I kept preaching that to them. And I did not discriminate. During that period of time that was when there were so many people who crawled in front of cars and marching and all that stuff. And the first three years was miserable, but I didn't let it get to me. And Stokely Carmichael called me one day and said he's coming after me.

He did?

He said, "You get ready. I'm coming after you."

I said, "I'm ready" and hung up. But he never did show up. Of course, you couldn't walk right in my office; you had to go through a reception area. I never did see him, but it unnerved me a little bit. But after three years something happened—it just quieted down. And I got the cooperation from then until I went out; I didn't have any more problems. I continued to go to their meetings and talk to them and try to be fair and I'm just as fair as I could be. I know one time they had a big party out there, and Martha and I had to go, and as we walked in they were singing, "We Shall Overcome." Walked in, sat down to eat and they brought a clear glass of water, full of water. Thought it was water. Turned out it was white lightning.

No! They gave that to the wrong guy.

I sipped it. Then I put it down.

And during that period, Martin Luther King, Jr., was killed when I was down there.

Oh.

I had my supervisors, the black supervisors. They were a big help to me during that period. They were at locations all over the city. Calling me and telling me what's happening. And I was relaying it to Herb Jenkins, the Chief of Police. On one call, I called him and told him Stokely Carmichael was in the Holiday Inn.

He said, "Where?"

I said on the fourth floor, room number whatever.

He said, "No, he's not."

I said, "Herb, he's down there. I know where he is and know what room he's in." And I told him again.

And he said, "Are you sure?"

I said I was. My black supervisors were telling me, see. And that night I was told that he went out there and was going to start a fire on Spring Street. One of the black supervisors said to him, "You start that fire, you'll never start another one."

And we didn't have any fires after Martin Luther King, Jr., was killed. And the next day when they brought him up there, I was standing out at the annex, out there in front of it, watching, a crowd of people, Bobby Kennedy, Nixon, all those people.

All the dignitaries.

All the dignitaries marching up there with him. And I was concerned then. I tell you, I was worried, being head of the post office. But by that time most people had begun to trust me, so I did pretty well. Got through that.

That's great. So that was enough time for your way of doing things to become apparent to people so they trusted you.

That's right. I got along pretty well.

You've been a witness to a lot of history and been involved in a lot of it.

Oh, yeah. I was right there involved in that. Of course, I had several shootings. Several killings inside the office while I was postmaster.

Inside the office.

I was called at home one night. Some fellow come in there and shot a woman on the work room floor. Of course, I went down there and they wouldn't let me in, the supervisors wouldn't let me get anywhere near it. But the police finally caught him two or three days later. He was up in the attic of some house someplace. They caught him, gave him life in prison. Then another supervisor was killed, had several shootings in there. There were a lot of domestic problems. Oh, I could write a book on that. It was awful.

Well, too, with such a large network of people and people who are out in the community and everything.

Yeah. So many—I'm not going to get into that.

Right, but that was a stressful part of your job.

The domestic problems—it was bad.

Martin Luther King, Sr.—I'd met Martin Luther King, Jr.—but this was Senior. Did I tell you about Senior?

No.

He used to come by every once in a while and see me. In 1965 the Voting Rights Act passed. We didn't have any women at the post office except secretaries. And all these black women who finished college passed this examination, got high on the register. We started hiring and ninety-nine out of a hundred were black women. And when one day, when Dr. King came in, one of my secretaries said, "Dr. King wants to see you." We talked and said the usual, glad to see you, and then he said, "Mr. Post-master, we got a problem, such a problem." He said, "You are tearing the black community apart."

"I am?"

"Yes," he said.

"What am I doing, Dr. King?"

He said, "These black women are coming up here and going to work and going home and kicking their husbands out, and it's tearing the black community apart."

"Dr. King," I said, "I can't do a thing about that."

"What do you mean you can't do a thing about that?"

"They're on top of the register, the top of the list." I said. "I have to hire one of the top three and the men are not up there, but the women are, and they're doing a good job."

"Gee," he said, "I'll just have to call the president."

I said, "Dr. King, go ahead."

He'd come out every two or three weeks; he'd come in and talk to me. He was a great old man. I liked him.

Really. That's interesting.

One time he came in—this was after Martin, Jr., got killed—and he said, "I have a problem."

"What's the problem, Dr. King?" I asked.

"Well, actually," he said, "it's Coretta; she's got the problem."

"What's her problem?"

He said, "Marty [Martin Luther King III] doesn't have a job and is giving his mama fits."

"What can I do?"

"I'll tell you," he said. "You could put him to work."

"All right," I said. "Yup, I'll put him to work."

They sent him up there, and I sent him to the personnel manager.

In three or four weeks, Martin Senior came back, and he said, "You done messed me up."

"What'd I do?"

"You done fired Marty."

"I what?"

"You fired Marty."

"How come you know that?"

"Marty told me," he said.

"Marty told you I fired him?"

"Yes."

"I didn't even know he was hired," I said. So I called the personnel manager. I had to get the story right quick. And he called me back in about fifteen minutes.

"The black supervisor at the annex fired him," he said. "And he told me why."

I told Dr. King. He said, "I guess he oughta been fired."

His grandfather saw the situation right away.

Yes. He understood exactly what had happened.

We had five regions in the United States Postal Service at the time I ended my career. And I was most fortunate. I guess I promoted, I had more of my people promoted to regional postmaster general than any other postmaster in the United States. I had Bill Campbell, Jerry Lee, Jackie Strange, Herv Daws, Johnny Thomas.

Of course now, when I got off the board, all the promotions were Northerners again. [Laughter]

Let me tell you how that came about, how I got some Southerners promoted. Once the postmaster general asked the board to approve an officer. And I said, "Where's he from?"

"Boston, Massachusetts," he said.

"Bill," I said, "why did you just promote somebody from Massachusetts?"

"Well," he said, "I thought that he was the best qualified."

"Did you know," I asked, "that you don't have an officer on your staff from the Southern Region of the United States?"

"I don't?" [Laughter]

"No, you don't," I said and then I asked, "Why?"

"I don't know," he said.

"Bill," I said, "you're the Postmaster General of the United States. I expect you to be fair and promote the most qualified person."

"I think this one is the most qualified."

"Well, I don't," I said, and we got into an argument, and I called him some nasty names. We were getting ready to have dinner, and I got up and left.

You did?

I should have said more. I went over and called the restaurant down-stairs and had them send me a meal. Next morning when the meeting of the board was about to begin, he walked up to me. I thought he was going to start it again. Instead, he said, "I want you to do something."

"What's that, Bill?"

"Give me the names of the ten most qualified people in the Southern Region."

"I'll give it to you in two hours." And I called Jerry Lee who was the controller of the Southern Region at that time, and told him to give me the ten names and I told him to put his name at the top of the list.

He said he'd call me back in ten minutes. It was over an hour, but he called me back, gave me those names, and I gave them to Bill. And then while he was postmaster general, one of them, Jackie Strange, became deputy postmaster general, the first woman ever to hold that position. All these people worked for me. I'm very proud of them.

Right. And so he didn't refer to your discussion, he just asked you for that list—

I'd called him bad names, and I was rough on him. Evidently, the boys got on him because he hadn't promoted anybody in the Southern Region. I didn't pursue it and didn't ask any questions. I could have been nice to him, but I was rough on him. But he worked for me; I was his boss.

Oh, right. You were on the Board of Governors. So then he opened up some of the higher positions—

Jerry Lee would come to the Washington District Controller and then become Assistant PMG of Finance; then he went to a new office and was Postmaster General of the New York Region; he went to Harvard and got his master's; then he come back and went to Chicago; he was Regional Postmaster General of the Chicago Region; then he went to the Southern Region. He had problems with transferring, and I brought him up in the Southern Region. That's where he retired. I still hear from Jerry from time to time.

Really? That's nice.

Well, I pushed him pretty good.

Well, I imagine developing talent was another rewarding part of your work, even as others had seen your potential and guided you.

I know I made mistakes, but I think I probably made sixty-one good ones and four or five bad. [Laughter]

One of those people who believed in you was Millsby Lane, right?

Yes. I don't know who owns it now, but he built that building, the Commerce Club. I went there at least once a month for dinner—I mean for lunch.

There does seem to have been a good group trying to develop leaders in Georgia.

Oh, yeah. Governor Carl Sanders called me one day and said, "George. I'll pick you up in five minutes."

"Well, why?" I asked.

"We're going to have a groundbreaking ceremony."

"Where's it at?" I asked. He told me it was out there off Interstate 75, and I said, "Okay."

So Mills and Governor Sanders picked me up and off we went. It turned out it was the groundbreaking ceremony for Braves Stadium, the old one. Mills, Carl Sanders, Ed Smith, and about twenty-five or thirty others were there.

You were there for a lot of Georgia history, Atlanta area history. You've had a life of wonderful happenings.

Oh, yes. The best things happened to me. My wife, she kept me going. She raised my children. Whatever they are is because of her; I was always on the move. For my whole life I'll never be able to repay her. And I don't forget those things.

CHAPTER 29

Do What's Right

How would you like people to think of you?

God-loving man. I try to live by "do unto others as you do unto your-self." Mama taught me that.

The Golden Rule.

The Golden Rule. That's right. I believe in that.

You seem to have, and you have had, a wonderful life.

Oh, yes.

George at his desk.

Do you remember when you were growing up thinking at all about what your life would be like?

Had no idea. [Laughter]

So it exceeded what you could have imagined.

Oh, yeah. Yeah, everything just, I don't know, fell in line.

What do you think has been your greatest accomplishment?

Well, I led the country in improving the postal service—at the Atlanta Postal Office, I think—I was number one for the last few years of my career. And, of course, that's not my greatest accomplishment. My greatest accomplishment was raising two of the finest sons in America.

Since we have talked a little bit about your career, let's consider one more aspect of that part of your life. You have led a large and important organization and been responsible for many employees. I know that you worked hard and that you believe in basing advancement for employees on performance. Could you talk a bit more on your thoughts on managing people? And on making an enterprise successful.

I believe in promoting people on merits, the best qualified person available. I don't care if man, female, black, white: it doesn't matter. I have followed that rule. And, you know, when I started out at Ft. McPherson in the data center, I went to Endicott, New York, IBM, they trained me a lot, had a lot of training.

Endicott was the headquarters of IBM Corporation. I went up there once or twice a year for several years. And then when I was in the data center I went to—what did they call it—the American Management Association. I had several weeks, eight or ten weeks in the American Management Association, which was a big help. So I've had training in that area. And I practiced what I learned. I used that. I promoted the people and demoted them because they didn't meet the expectation, but then once they qualified, I reappointed them. And the records show I did that. And, of course, I had a lot of problems on charges of discrimination during that period—you know what was going on back in those periods. But I never was convicted of anything; I always come out clean. I was lucky. But I tried to be fair.

You were promoting on merit—

On merit, that's right. The best qualified person available. And I never did believe in talking down to my staff. I always listened to them. That didn't mean I always agreed with them. Sometimes I would, sometimes I wouldn't. If I didn't agree with them, we did it my way. But if I did agree with them, I changed. We did it their way if I agreed with them. Two heads are better than one. You have to listen to your staff. If you don't, you're not going to be successful. I don't think any man can run an organization by himself. Because everybody—if you're in a top job—there are a lot of people underneath saying, "He don't know what he's doing." Rumors, you've heard all these rumors. Don't pay any attention to them. Do what's right. You'll be all right.

Another thing in terms of the organization, let's say you're leaving the office when you were postmaster, and you're leaving Atlanta or you're home on a Saturday and you're thinking about your work. How would you imagine it? Would you be looking at the whole organization, or at bits and pieces? How does one cope with dealing with an organization that size when you're the person at the top who's responsible?

Well, first of all, when I left my office in the evening, I left my job there. I didn't bring it home with me. I didn't bring my work home with me. Because you can get sick doing that. You've got to leave it alone. And if I wanted to know something, I had a number to call. If it was personnel, I'd call my personnel manager, and he'd give me a report. So I'd call the right person, and I'd forget it until I went back to work.

You would.

Yeah. Because you can't take your work home with you. You will not be successful by taking your work home. I never did that. And when I was on the Board of Governors, the material I got in, I reviewed it here so I'd be prepared when I went to the next board meeting to discuss it. But as far as worrying about it, I didn't worry about it. I wouldn't live this long if I had.

That's good. That's good advice.

Now Endicott (IBM) taught me that. They taught me that. Don't take your work home with you.

CHAPTER 30

Family

What's the most important thing in your life right now?

My family. Now, has been, and always will be. Well, I'd say my family; I've already said that the most important thing in life is the Lord, family, country, and politics in that order. And I guess that applies to me pretty much.

Let's talk about some general topics, but maybe in the back of your mind you could almost feel like you might be talking to your children and grandchildren, or just people in general, from your vantage point right now. What are your thoughts regarding education?

Education, oh, you can't get enough of it now. The world has changed so much. If you don't have a good education, you're not going to make it. You're not going to be as fortunate, as lucky as I was. You've got to have an education today, and the more education you get the better you're going to be able to provide for yourself and your family. You've got to do that. If you don't, why you're going to be a day laborer, minimum wage.

And what about choosing and managing a career?

Well, I feel like that you're going to have to work at something you like and enjoy. If you don't, there again, you won't be successful. If you're not happy with your work, and you dread to go to work, that's not going to work. Just like my last assignment at the postal service in Memphis. I didn't enjoy that. I couldn't wait to get out of there.

And you got out.

Yes, I got out. It was nothing productive. You'd sit there and talk about something, but you couldn't carry it out. Every job I had before then you'd talk about something, then you decide,and then you do it. But that regional job, that was a bunch of hooey. I didn't like that.

What advice would you give a young person about money, money management?

As soon as you possibly can, start saving some money. I was pretty old before I was able to accumulate because I didn't make a lot of money. Of course, if you don't, you're going to be hurting in your old age, and you're going to be calling on your children, and you don't want that. I never believed in that. You got to provide for your later years in life.

About how to raise children?

My wife can answer that better than I can. She did a wonderful job. She did a wonderful job.

And how about love and marriage? What kind of advice would you give a young person?

Well, you've got to be sure you're ready, and you pick the right one. There's too many divorces this day and time. I don't know. That's, I guess, the biggest decision you make in life: picking your partner.

I guess you've touched in a lot of different ways throughout our interviews about your philosophy of life, but is there anything else you want to say about the philosophy of how to live?

Oh, nothing except live the Golden Rule. That's number one as far as I'm concerned. And provide for your family. Put your family first.

Well, I have this question but I think I already know the answer. What do you think your saddest moment has been?

When I lost my mama and daddy. And my brother. You know, my brother next to me was mentally retarded slightly. My other brother, Donald—I got a call one day from Mama, saying he was in jail up in Dallas. So I called the judge. He took my call.

How old were you at this point?

I was probably twenty-seven. And they had caught him playing poker under a bridge, he and a bunch of boys, playing poker under a bridge in Dallas. And the judge told me – Hal Hutchinson was the judge—he said, "I want him out of Paulding County. I don't want him in Paulding County anymore." He said, "That's the only way I'll let him out of jail."

So I went up and got him and brought him to Atlanta, moved him in with me and put him in Brown High School. He went there several years, and in his senior year, I don't know why he did this—Korean War was going on—he quit and joined the army. That was a sad time for me. But he served in Europe; he was a prisoner in the Korean War, and he escaped. He got out and started the Northeast Heating and Air Conditioning Company here in Atlanta. He was very successful, doing all right. But I don't know what the problems were between him and his wife, but he never did tell me, and I'm glad I didn't know about it. But one night somebody, my sister, called and said he'd shot his wife and killed himself.

Oh, no.

He went home, and she'd called the police, and they drove in the drive-way. That's when he shot her. I didn't get over that easy. Great young fellow, smart. He heated and air conditioned big hotels downtown, the big stuff. That was his second wife. He and his first wife divorced. But I don't know. He was a good bit older than her. I don't know the details.

Right and there are things in your life that—

Wouldn't do any good. I never asked questions. Ronnie, my son, Ronnie settled his estate. He wouldn't let me get involved in it.

That was good protection, which you needed.

That's right. But that was hard.

All the things we've talked about—is there anything you've thought about that you'd like to add or just something that we haven't talked about that you—

There's something I, you know, back when I was I guess from the time I was six years old until I was fifteen, we, my dad was one of the largest farmers in Paulding County, and we had tenants who helped us. And in the springtime we always would come to Atlanta to buy goods and services. And one time he was going to bring me with him. We got up at four o'clock in the morning, hitched up to the two-horse wagon, and come to Atlanta. We bought several barrels of flour, a hundred pounds of pinto beans; I don't know—a lot, a big bag of sugar, coffee, a hoop of cheese, and some salt. Staples that you had to have.

Then after the wagon was loaded, he went in and bought a little hoop, a little round thing full of white fish, salty. I couldn't eat them. But he always loved those little fish. Mama would fry them for breakfast. But we left, that time I went with him, it was thirty miles from where we lived in Dallas to Peter's Street. We left at four o'clock in the morning; it was ten that night when we got back. I'd like to froze. Just he and I on that wagon. I remember that. But that's the only time I rode with him on that wagon. But he did that every spring when he was farming big time. And after I left home, he didn't have any more tenants. Just he and my sisters and my brother helping him, didn't farm as large until he quit farming and went to work with Lockheed. But he always had a garden. My dad.

So that's a day that stands out in your memory. Being with him all day and—

Oh, yeah, I won't forget that trip. It was a long way to ride in an old two-horse wagon. [Laughter] But there were a lot of two-horse wagons at

George's father, William Maddox Camp.

Peter's Street that time. You know how it is out there, west of Five Points. That's where people buy, where there are wholesale groceries, where the farmers come in and buy stuff.

Thirty miles didn't go by quite as fast in that wagon, that mode of transportation.

Yeah, yeah.

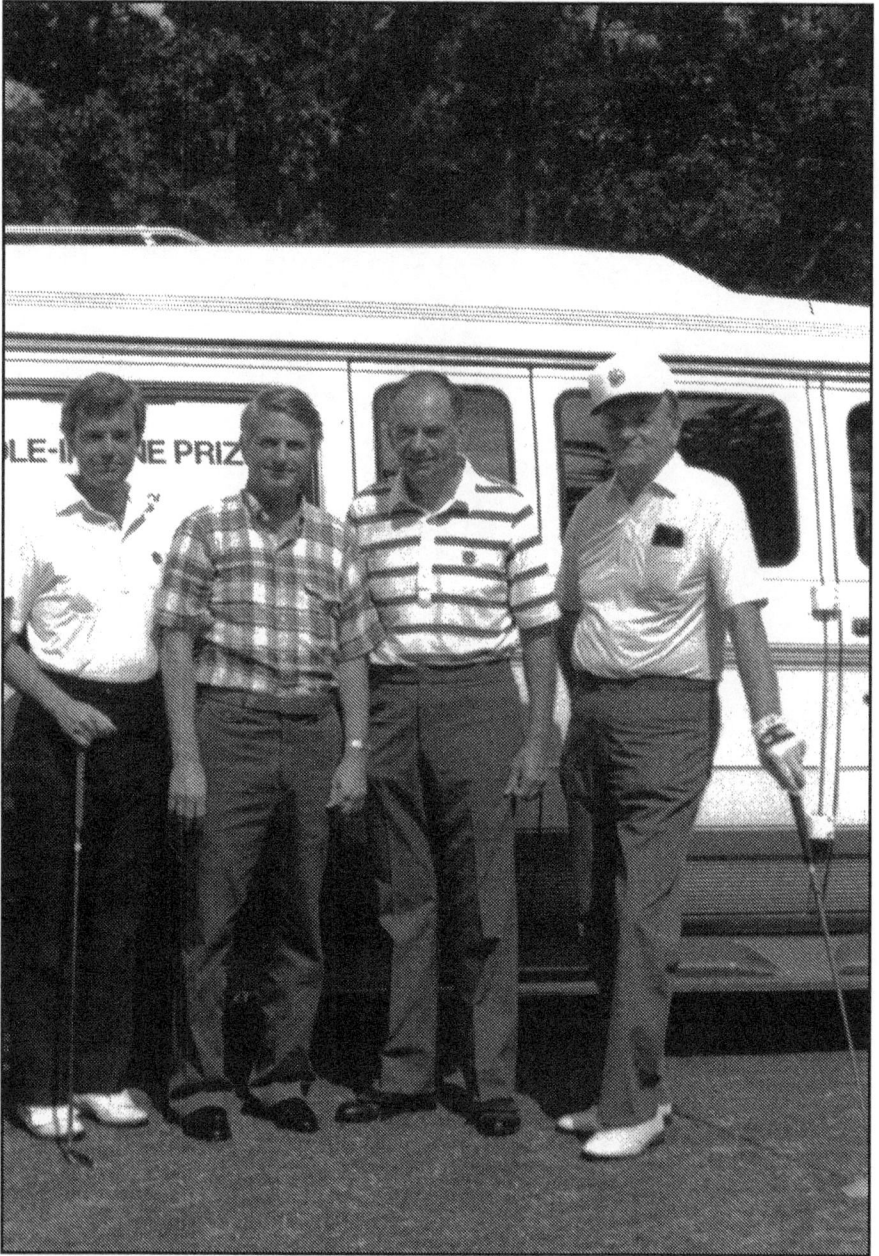

George, Zell Miller, and friends at a tournament quite a few years ago. Golf is still a beloved pastime.

CHAPTER 31

Satisfied and Happy

Let's discuss some specifics from the past and present. Do you have any health problems that are considered hereditary?

Not that I know of.

Do you do anything now regularly for exercise?

Play golf. Love golf. I used to play two or three days a week, but not now – because of the conditions here at home I can't get away all that much.

But you're still playing.

Oh yes. Played yesterday.

Where do you play?

Different places. I did belong to Brookfield for twenty years. Then I went to Polo Club, but I got tired of paying three or four hundred dollars a month just playing once a week. So I get out. You can go just about anywhere now and play for fifty dollars. I play at different places.

Do you have people you play with?

Oh, yeah. We have a bunch of people in my church. Ten or twelve, fourteen of them.

And you love the game?

Yeah, long as I win. [Laughter] I don't like getting beat. And I won yesterday.

So you're in a good mood. You look like you're in an especially good mood today. Well, that's great. That's wonderful. On the down side, have you ever been the victim of a crime?

No, I don't believe I have. Well, when I was on the Board of Governors, I was not a victim, but one of my [fellow] board members was a victim. He got caught trying to line up something to get rich. And I was inspected; I mean they really checked me out.

Oh, that's right.

But as far as, I don't know, I've never paid a speeding ticket in my life. I paid a parking ticket one time. Been lucky there because I've deserved some. I just wasn't caught.

But you still haven't had one.

Oh, Ronnie and I were coming back from Florida one time, and he was ahead of me, and the state patrol stopped us and give him a ticket and me a ticket and that's the only time I've ever been stopped on the street. But I, maybe I shouldn't say this, but I took those tickets to Carl Sanders the next morning. I'd forgotten about that. Carl was governor then. [Laughter]

So he took care of that for you.

Let's see. Is there anything you've always wanted to do but haven't?

I don't know. I've always been able to do just pretty much what I wanted to. Real lucky. Of course, there's always things that you'd like to have or like to do, but nothing that pried on my mind. I'm satisfied and happy. I've lived a good life. I have no complaints.

There's an old song that says, "satisfied, tickled, too." That might describe you.

That's right.

Let's see. Some more general questions. We talked about, say, how your childhood and your parents' childhood were rather similar versus the sort of break there where it became much different. How in general do you think the world is different now from when you were a child?

Well, it's a lot different. I can only speak to my condition, my situation. My boys when they were growing up, they didn't have chores to do, except sometimes cut the grass or rake leaves or something like that. They didn't have to get out and cut wood, haul it in, pick cotton, and do all these other things. Most children don't have to work today like we did in those days. I don't know whether that's good or bad. But you have more money, and you can provide for your family better. Better clothes. Involved in more sports activities and things to do, and you go on vacation. When I was a boy, we never had a vacation. I was twenty-five years old before I ever had a vacation in my life. But these children they get to see ocean sometimes before they realize what it is. Go where they want to—it's a completely different world. And I'm glad it's that way. I'm glad it's that way.

But what of the old kinds of principles, though, still apply do you think, some of the things that worked for you, clearly, still would work for people today with a little different twist?

Well, things that we did. When we had company, the older people ate first; children eat what's left. Today it doesn't work that way. Children eat first and the older people eat last. And another thing—you didn't dare not say "yes, sir" and "no, sir" to a man and "yes, ma'am" to a lady. You didn't dare not to do that. Do you hear that often today?

No, sir.

You don't hear that often today. But you did then. You did then.

There are some movements in education now of going back to that at least in the classroom, saying that it makes for a better atmosphere.

I think it does. It would take a while to go back to it. Now when my boys were coming up, when they were young, they did that. I taught them. And I would think they might do that now to people older than them. But when they were little they did. They'd say "yes, ma'am" to their mama. I don't think they do that no more.

You've mentioned a number of people who had a positive impact on your life or made good things happen for you. For instance, the thing about you never applied for a job really. But can you pick one or two as having maybe been the most important or—

Of course, my daddy's first. My daddy meant everything to me. He taught me common sense, I guess. Taught me how to work. Taught me how to make a living. How to go about things. And I worked for several different people, but the man I worked for that did the most for me was Mr. A. C. Lawrence. In the postal data center. He was tough and rough and mean. He'd cuss you out in a minute. But I'd always laugh at him and then he'd get mad because I was laughing at him. But he's the man that promoted me to be in charge of the data center. He's the man that called me down there one day and said he wanted me to be the postmaster of Atlanta. I never had thought about it. Never dreamed about it.

He was watching you, and he saw that you could do it—

And after I retired from the postal service, he's the man who wanted me on the Postal Board of Governors. He's the man that got the ball rolling. Not me. I didn't do nothing. He did it. And, of course, you wanted three, and another one is Dick Russell, Senator Dick Russell. Senator Dick Russell was one of the finest men I ever met in my life. And I had dinner with him and Margaret Chase Smith and Senator Dirksen. They would sit there and fight and when they came to an agreement, one of them would say, "Now, do you think that's best for the country?"

And the Senate would vote the way they decided. Because they were powerful men. Dirksen and Russell were powerful men and we don't have that anymore, I don't think. We may have, but I don't know about it.

Senator Russell was a great man.

He was good to you, and you wouldn't have taken that position—you were worried about taking the postmaster job—without his support.

I didn't know I was going to get it that morning I talked to him. I didn't know it was going to be announced that day. And everybody's running around in that building like—some of them were running up and down that elevator, and I was working, telling people what to do and all that business. And the paper comes out and somebody brought the paper in and showed me.

I'd like to have seen your face then.

Of course, I was happy about it.

Well, what's left? What was the most stressful experience do you think that you ever lived through? Maybe we could do it in terms of your career.

Probably when they called me and wanted me to come to work for the postal service and run the data center. I had a guy named Jim Osburn, that was Mr. Lawrence's assistant. He'd graduated from college, had a master's degree, brilliant, brilliant young guy. And he and I were trying to upgrade and update this data center. And I tried to stay with him. That was the hardest thing I'd ever done. But I did.

Keeping up with—he'd already been there and established—

He was brilliant. He was brilliant. I know when we were programming the 650, that's the first big computer and, of course, I had no problem with conventional programming—learned that easy. And they came out with a system of programming they referred to as SOAP. Well, I read that book, and I couldn't understand it.

What was it called?

SOAP. I've forgotten what that meant. But he didn't understand it either. We both studied that thing for three months and finally one morning he come in, he called me, and said, "I've conquered it. I know what to do." And he sat down with me and in fifteen minutes, I knew it.

Really? So he had a breakthrough, and he shared it with you.

But that's the last programming I did, was SOAP, and everything's changed now. People say that the computer says it won't work; the computer tells you what you tell it to, and it doesn't make mistakes. I know that. But back in my early days, I knew exactly what you had to know, how it was working. Of course everything's a branching operation. Yes or no, everything about it was yes or no, still that way. But it operates in nanoseconds now, I think.

That was the most stressful and the hardest time that I—went through a period there, six or eight months—sometimes I'd go to work on Monday morning and wouldn't come home until Tuesday night or Wednesday. Working. Both of us. He and I both. He was right there with me. Martha'd phone me at two or three o'clock in the morning: "When you coming home?" The boys were little then. That was rough. That's the hardest assignment I ever had, I guess.

How about what makes you laugh? You laugh a lot—

I'm lucky. I was lucky in my life. I have a good life, enjoy myself.

There are a lot of things that can make you smile in this life.

Oh, yeah. Oh, yeah. Why people go around with a sad look on their face—they've got everything to be thankful for if they're walking around. I don't know if there's anything I could feel bad about now if something happened to me today. I've been so fortunate and so lucky. So blessed. So blessed. I've been blessed beyond all means.

THE END

www.ingramcontent.com/pod-product-compliance
Lightning Source LLC
Chambersburg PA
CBHW020517100426
42813CB00030B/3280/J